Change Management

the People Side of Change

*An introduction to change management from the
editors of the Change Management Learning Center*

www.change-management.com

Jeffrey M. Hiatt
Timothy J. Creasey

Prosci Learning Center Publications

First edition

Printed in the United States of America

Library of Congress Control Number: 2003111671

Hiatt, Jeffrey M., Creasey, Timothy J.
   Change Management: the People Side of Change

   p.   cm.

      ISBN 1-930885-18-0 paperback
      ISBN 1-930885-19-9 hardcover

      1. Organizational change - Management 2. Project
      management 3. Psychology - Change. I. Title

      HD58.8   2003
      658.4'06--dc20

Prosci Research
Loveland, Colorado, USA

Cover design by Larissa Carlson

The paper used in this publication meets the requirements of the American National Standard for Permanence of Paper for Printed Library Materials Z39.49-1984.

Volume discounts and direct orders are available from Prosci Research by calling 970-203-9332 or by visiting www.change-management.com

Advance praise for *Change Management: the People Side of Change*

"Great book! This book takes the sometimes overly academic work around change management and makes it easy, understandable and <u>actionable</u>."

> Laura Roethe, Change Management Practice Leader,
> CUNA Mutual Group

"The principles illustrated in the book are timeless and appropriate to any condition where things are not static. In fact, they are based upon great quantities of common sense — so much so that their utilization is not common."

> Kim A. Kennedy, General Manager,
> Industrial Operations, Blue Diamond

"This is a must read. Recognizing the need for change and effectively leading the correct changes may be the most important leadership role for today's executives. In today's competitive and uncertain economic environment, change competency may be the key to success."

> E.H. (Gene) Sherman, Founder and CEO,
> Baynard Cove Group

"Great book on change management — especially the ideas presented on integrating the organizational and individual elements of change management. The book has forced me to look at change management in a new way!"

> Susan L. Schleusner, Project Manager,
> Storage Technology Corporation

"A wonderful primer for change management. Every organization, both public and private, should view this text as required reading before implementing major change."

> Dr. James Johnson, Adjunct Faculty,
> Regis University

Contents

CHAPTER 1

Why manage change?

As editors of the Change Management Learning Center, we have analyzed research data from more than 1,000 companies involved in large-scale changes. We talk daily with project leaders and managers. We write weekly articles and tutorials on managing the people side of change. We review new books in this field of study. What we observe more than anything else is the need for easy-to-apply concepts and practical guidelines for managing change. Yet, up to now, a straightforward introduction to change management has not been available.

When finished with this book, you will have a basic context for change management, know why it is important and understand how it is used. As a business manager, you will be more effective as a change leader and sponsor of change. Specifically, you will be able to prevent and manage resistance to change, minimize productivity loss, avoid unnecessary turnover and increase the probability that your business changes produce the desired results.

Why manage change?

Whether you are an executive, supervisor, coach, consultant, project team leader or manager of any type where your job is to manage people, you likely have experienced resistance to change from employees. However, you may not recognize the role that you can play in preventing that resistance and leading change. Most managers do not make this connection until they have personally experienced failure in an important change project.

"I should have communicated better."

"Next time I will involve more people."

"If the CEO had just been more public in his support."

"I was undermined by managers who felt threatened by this change and did not understand the vision."

These common reflections by business leaders after an unsuccessful initiative have one common theme: each represents a failure to manage the people side of change. They are not alone. In a general study[1] of companies implementing major business changes, 327 project leaders, consultants and managers answered the following question about their project overall:

"If you had the chance to do it again, what would you do differently?"

The most common response was:

"Utilize an effective and planned
change management program."

Surprisingly, these study participants did not emphasize design or technology issues. They did not say they lacked vision or an understanding of the marketplace. The most common barrier to success was a lack of change management. They fell short when managing the people side of change and encountered:

1. Managers who were unwilling to assign the needed resources to the project or would not allow their representative adequate time to participate

2. Managers who filtered out important messages or started negative conversations about the change

3. Employees who became distracted and lost interest in their current work responsibilities thereby impacting overall productivity and customers

4. Valued employees who left the organization

5. More people taking sick leave or not showing up for work

6. Unforeseen obstacles to the change that seemingly appeared from nowhere

7. A lack of funding for the change

In other words, things did not go exactly as planned. The unexpected happened. Not managing the people side of change impacted their success and introduced risk into their projects.

Change management can not only mitigate these business risks, but in many cases avoid them entirely. Business leaders have the potential to not only manage resistance once it appears, but to prevent it in the first place. Unfortunately, many business leaders and project teams do not appreciate their role in managing the people side of change until after resistance impacts the success of their change.

Two case studies show the potential consequences of not managing the people side of change. These case studies were selected because they highlight two common leadership mistakes: first, believing that change management is someone else's job; second, ignoring the people side of change until major resistance stalls a project or causes the project to fail.

Case Study 1 - The Reluctant CEO

To reduce cost and improve customer service, a financial group wanted to consolidate its customer contact centers across several divisions. A consultant was hired to support the effort and to prepare implementation plans. The project no more than began when rumor spread through several departments that this organizational change was not good for the company. Supervisors and key managers in the existing customer care centers began resisting the change. In some cases they would not show up for design reviews or miss key decision-making meetings. Information requested by the consultant and the design team was withheld or half-complete. At breaks and around the coffee pot, employees complained about potential leadership changes. Both employees and managers were distracted from their day-to-day work and productivity suffered. Key managers were rumored to quit if the change was implemented. The consulting firm met with the CEO, repeatedly warning that this resistance would undermine his change and would ultimately begin to affect customers. The CEO, however, was reluctant to become personally involved. He viewed change management as the job of his project team and the consultant, and not the responsibility of the head of the company. After several months of difficulties and delays, the consultants finally declared the consolidation in jeopardy.

With the project at a stand-still, the CEO requested an emergency briefing with his leadership team. To prepare for this status report, the consultants conducted interviews with key managers throughout each department. They quickly identified a manager in an existing customer care center who viewed his job at risk with the potential change. Arguments against the change initiated by this manager were spreading throughout the ranks. His supervisors were the same people who were presumably threatening to leave the organization.

Even armed with this information, the CEO remained reluctant to take definitive action. The only recourse at this stage was reassignment or termination of this manager. Both options could have negative fall-out for the company and the affected manager. The CEO was faced with a stalled project and a potentially lose-lose decision for a long-tenured manager.

In this case, the CEO made two mistakes that are common in major changes. The first was to assume that change management was someone else's responsibility. In a change management benchmarking study with 288 companies,[2] the number one research finding related to

an executive's role in change is active and visible sponsorship at every phase of the project. The second mistake
the CEO made was not managing resistance when it first
surfaced. Resistance to change can spread like wildfire
when not managed effectively. Waiting, in this case, only
resulted in a more difficult situation later on.

Case Study 2 - Stripes and Tar

The president of a business association had facilities
maintenance as part of his overall responsibilities. The
association included multiple businesses that each had
condominiums in a single large office complex. The president of the association decided that the parking lot needed resurfacing and new striping. He arranged for a local
contractor to do the work.

One day the construction company showed up at the
office complex and started blocking off the parking lot.
The contractor was getting his equipment ready and was
trying to clear the lot of cars when disgruntled business
owners confronted his workers. The business owners
wanted to know what was happening, why it was happening and who authorized the work. Not happy with the
uninformed answers from the contractor and the immediate demands to remove the cars from the lot, the business
owners instructed the contractor to pack up his equipment and leave. Since the president was not on site to
resolve conflicts, the contractor had no choice but to aban-
don the job.

Even when the president finally intervened later in
the day, enough business owners were upset about the
unknown financial impact and the disruptive process that
the contractor never returned to resurface the parking lot.

In this case, the association president knew what needed to be done, took charge and moved ahead. The change was small, and in terms of maintenance, he was doing the right thing for the association. However, the president neglected to make the business owners *aware* that the lot needed resurfacing as part of normal maintenance. He did not *communicate* the financial benefit to the association and therefore the financial benefit to each business owner. Finally, the president did not inform the business owners about *how* and *when* the work would be done, and what the business owners needed to do to support the project. The result was resistance from the business owners, who, in this case, had sufficient authority to stop the work. The association president simply ignored the people side of the change and the project failed.

Both complex and simple changes can fail. With many projects, the evidence of failure from not managing the people side of change is not as black and white as the absence of new blacktop with freshly painted white lines. Failure can come in many forms including project delays, loss of valued employees, significant declines in productivity and customer dissatisfaction.

In Case Study 1, the CEO did not think that managing change was part of his job. It was not until a crisis emerged that the CEO became involved. Mid-level and senior managers can make this same mistake. They often look upward, thinking that change management is someone else's responsibility. In Case Study 2, the association president viewed the change as small and simple, a change that he did not think required change management.

Why do many business leaders believe that managing the people side of change is not their job? At the onset of a new change, managers are typically focused on issues besides change management. Executives want the change to happen as soon as possible. Their focus is on results. They are aware of the business issues facing the organization and are accountable for financial performance. When a change is needed, they want action quickly. Their primary concerns are:

- What is the required investment?

- How will this change impact our financial performance?

- What is the return on this investment?

- When can the change be completed?

- How much improvement will be realized?

- How will this change impact our customers?

If the answers to these questions are favorable, then the directive to a project manager or project team is typically "let's get it done." The executive's focus is not on change management.

The perspective of front-line employees (and in many cases their supervisors and managers within the organization) is very different. They generally do not have detailed insights into the business strategy and financial performance of the business, nor do they share the same accountabilities as business leaders. Many employees cannot connect what they do everyday with the performance of the company; therefore, it is difficult to convince them to change based only on company performance.

Their focus is on the day-to-day job. Serving customers, processing orders, getting their work done – these are their primary areas of interest. When a change is made, their primary concerns are:

- What will this change mean to me?

- Will I have a job?

- Do I have the needed skills and knowledge to succeed in the new environment?

To complete the picture, consider the consultants or project team who encounter both of these different perspectives yet have the job to design and implement the change. They are accountable to the business leaders that authorized the change, yet must work with employees to implement the change successfully.

Employees, the project team and executives have different priorities, different knowledge sets and different motivations. Change brings these different priorities, knowledge sets and motivations together in a potentially volatile mix. Employees feel threatened. Executives expect results. The project team is caught in the middle. The business enters a period in which the risk of productivity loss, customer dissatisfaction and employee turnover increases dramatically. It is at this critical juncture that change management plays a crucial role for business success.

To survive in today's marketplace, a business must constantly examine its performance, strategy, processes and systems to understand what changes need to be made. At the same time, an organization must also understand the implications of a new business change on its employees, given their culture, values, history and capacity for change. Employees ultimately perform the new day-to-day activities and make the new processes and systems come to life in the business. Change management is about managing people in a changing environment so that business changes are successful and the desired business results are realized.

The challenge for today's leaders

These two views of change, the top-down executive's view and the bottom-up employee's view, create two distinct challenges for managing change. These two challenges can be referred to as organizational change management (from the manager's perspective) and individual change management (from the employee's perspective). Both are skills that today's leaders need for success.

Organizational change management is the perspective of business leadership from the top looking down into the organization. The focus is around broad change management practices and skills that will help the organization understand, accept and support the needed business change. The emphasis is on communications, training and the overall culture or value system of the organization.

Individual change management is the management of change from the perspective of the employees. They are the ones who ultimately must implement the change. The focus for individual change management is around the tools and techniques to help employees through the transition. Managers and supervisors must provide the coaching required to help individuals understand their role and the decisions they make in the change process.

Overall, change management is about helping people

through change. It is the process, tools and techniques for proactively managing the people side of change in order to achieve the desired business results.

Getting up to speed

Change management is the application of many different ideas from the fields of engineering, business and psychology. As changes in organizations have become more frequent and a necessity for survival, the body of knowledge known as "change management" has also grown to encompass more skills and knowledge from each of these fields of study. While this may be a good trend overall, the result for many business leaders is growing confusion about what change management really is.

The purpose of this book is to bring the meaning of change management into focus. Written for executives, managers and consultants, this book will provide you with a solid understanding of the principles and processes around managing change in today's competitive environment. Case studies, examples and even a personal exercise will help bring the concepts to life.

A different change management definition

The software and IT community have long used the term "change management" to refer to the processes and systems of managing software and hardware revisions (also referred to as change control). If you conduct a search on an internet search engine under the term "change management," you will find mixed listings. Some listings are for change management as defined in this book. Other listings are for software and hardware change control. This is an unfortunate collision of two fields of study using the same terminology to refer to two completely different topics. However, the IT community is often involved in major business change projects, and therefore as a practitioner you must be sure that your team understands change management as it is being applied for your project.

Moving forward

Before jumping into the models for individual change management and organizational change management, we have devoted a chapter to the principles and theories that contribute to the current thinking on managing change. These principles will provide a foundation for the models presented later in this book.

References

1. Prosci. (2002). *Business Process Reengineering Benchmarking Report*. Loveland, CO: Learning Center Publications.

2. Prosci. (2003). *Best Practices in Change Management*. Loveland, CO: Learning Center Publications.

CHAPTER 2

Theories and principles of change management

Most change management models in use today are in the form of a process or set of steps. These processes or activity lists were developed through trial and error, and are based on experiences of experts in the field of change management. In some cases these experts have created a standard process based on their consultancy models. These experts often use the same processes with their clients that are published in their books, articles and training materials.

Unfortunately, the underlying lessons and principles that resulted in these change management processes are not always clear. In many cases the principles are not even discussed as part of the resulting model. In a sense, what you learn is the *how* but not the *why*. The years of practical experience and knowledge that formed the base for these processes are not readily available to business managers.

A story about a young man watching his mother prepare a roast illustrates the importance of this point. Each time his mother cooks a pot roast, she cuts two inches off each end of the roast.

The son asked, "Mom, why do you cut the ends off?"

"I don't know," replied Mom, "that is the way Grandma always did it."

The son decided to investigate with a series of phone calls first to Grandma, then to Great Grandma. Grandma said she did it just the way Great Grandma showed her. After talking with Great Grandma, the son discovered that she cut the ends off the roast because her oven and cooking pan were too small, and she had to cut the ends off to make it fit.

Mom and Grandma knew the *how* – cutting two inches off each side of the roast – but not the *why* – because the original pan was too small. Ovens and pans are larger now and it is no longer necessary to shorten the roast.

Understanding the *why* makes you better at doing the *how*. Change management is not a matter of simply following steps. Since no two changes are exactly alike, following a recipe for change management is not enough. The right approach will be specific to the situation. If you do not understand the *why*, changes can fail even when standard processes are followed. Research with hundreds of project teams has shown that a one-size-fits-all approach is not sufficient. To be effective at leading change, you will need to customize and scale your change management efforts based on the unique characteristics of the change and the attributes of the impacted organization.

To accomplish this customization, an understanding of the psychology of change and key guiding principles is vital. You will then be able to work with many change management methodologies and adjust your approach according to the size and nature of the change, ultimately making your change a success.

Primary principles for change management

The guiding principles that will impact your change management activities are shown in Figure 1. The overview of principles and ideas presented here is not intended to be an in-depth psychological analysis. Rather, the focus will be on the key insights from these principles that impact effective application of change management. Case studies are used to illustrate key messages including how one million dollars in cash served as a change management tool.

Figure 1 - Primary change management principles

Principle 1 - Senders and receivers

Every change can be viewed from the perspective of a sender and a receiver. A *sender* is anyone providing information about the change. A *receiver* is anyone being given information about the change.

Senders and receivers are often not in a *dialogue* at the onset of a change. They often talk right past one another as shown in Figure 2. What a sender says and what a receiver hears are often two very different messages.

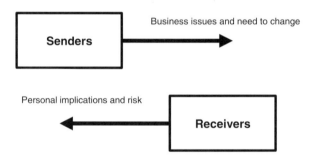

Figure 2 - Sender and receiver disconnect

For example, if a supervisor sits down with an employee to discuss a major restructuring project within the company, the supervisor may be enthusiastic and positive. She may cover all the key messages including the business reasons for change, the risk of not changing and the urgency to change the organization to remain competitive. The supervisor may even emphasize that this is a challenging and exciting time. However, when the employee discusses this change at home over dinner, the key messages to her family are often:

"I may not have a job."

"The company is having trouble."

The supervisor may spend 95% of the conversation talking about the business and 5% talking about the implications to the employee. At home, the employee is more likely to spend 95% of the time talking about the impact on her personally and 5% on the issues facing the company.

The consequence is that much of the key business information communicated by the supervisor to the employee in this first conversation is not heard. It is overshadowed by concerns related to job security and fear about change.

Many factors influence what an employee hears and how that information is interpreted. Examples of these factors include:

- Other career or educational plans

- Situations at home or with personal relationships

- Their past experience with other changes at work

- What they have heard from their friends or work colleagues

- Their current performance on the job

- Whether or not they trust or respect the sender

Now multiply these factors by the number of employees who are the receivers of change messages, and add even more variables as each person could have a different agenda. You can begin to appreciate the challenge faced by many businesses as they communicate the change to their employees.

Preferred senders

Based on Prosci's change management research study with 288 organizations,[1] employees prefer two primary senders of change messages. Not surprisingly, they also prefer specific message content from each of these senders. Immediate supervisors are the preferred senders of messages related to personal impact including:

- How does this impact me?

- How does this impact our group?

- How will this change my day-to-day responsibilities?

When it comes to personal issues, receivers want to hear from someone they know and work with regularly, namely their supervisor.

CEOs or executive leaders are the preferred senders of messages related to business issues and opportunities including:

- What are the external customer and competitor factors driving this change?

- What are the current issues facing the business?

- Are there other marketplace drivers?

- What are the financial risks if we do not change?

When it comes to business issues and why the change is needed, receivers want to hear from the person in charge.

The sender and receiver concept is very relevant to the actions taken by change management teams, project teams and business leaders in the change management process. Typically, executives, project teams and supervisors are the *senders* of key messages. They follow a prescribed communications plan to share information about the change. These communication activities are part of organizational change management.

In some cases, however, managers do not assess what their employees actually heard, nor do they understand how that information was processed. They merely complete a communication activity, check off a box, and move on to the next activity. A poor assumption is that *"employees heard just what I said and understood exactly what I meant."*

More likely, employees heard only a fraction of what was said, and their translation of that message will be unique to their personal situation. Some employees may have heard more than what was said, or will make up answers to questions that they do not understand. The answers they make up are typically worse than reality.

Realizing that *what receivers hear and what senders say is not always the same* is the first step to understanding that change management cannot be reduced to a set of activities or steps. Managers must not only be clear in their communications, they must also *listen* to employees to understand how their messages are being received. Change management communication is only effective when employees have internalized the change messages and can begin the transition process.

Principle 2 - Resistance and comfort

Change management practitioners and business leaders often underestimate the level of comfort with the current state. In the book *Changing the Way We Change*, LaMarsh refers to this as the power of the present.

> *"The present is so powerful that at times it seems to defy logic."*[2]

The natural and normal reaction to change is resistance. Every individual has a threshold for how much change they can absorb based on:

- Their personal history

- Current events in their life

- Current changes at work

- How much other change is going on

Moreover, some employees will resist the change no matter what. Even when individuals can align the change with their self-interest and belief system, the uncertainty of success and fear of the unknown can block change.

Resistance to change can spread and become a significant barrier to success. Although initial resistance is a natural reaction to change, ongoing resistance left unattended can become a threat to the business and to customers. A critical component of any good change management process will be a program to proactively manage resistance.

In the first case study with the reluctant CEO, a senior manager of one of the existing customer care centers was a severe and persistent source of resistance. To make matters more complex, this company had a long history and reputation of taking care of employees and building a sense of "family" in the workplace. Most of the leadership team had been with the company for 20 years or more. Taking decisive action with this manager was therefore problematic and for months no action was taken.

Finally, the impact of this single manager's behavior on the project and on the future of the change was so visible and contagious that the CEO had to intervene. If effective change management had been used with this manager at the initiation of the project, or if the resistance to change had been addressed earlier, most, if not all, of the negative consequences could have been avoided.

The three critical and relevant lessons for change management practitioners related to employee resistance and the power of comfort with the status quo are:

- Do not react to resistance with surprise; expect it and plan for it. Be patient with individuals as they work their way through the change process.

- Assess resistance not only from an individual's natural aversion or dislike to change, but also based on how much other change is going on (what is the capacity for more change).

- Persistent and prolonged resistance from middle management (or anyone in the organization) that is not addressed by executive sponsors can threaten a project and compromise success. Sponsors must determine and understand why the resistance exists and deal with the root cause.

Principle 3 - Authority for change

In Prosci's research on business process reengineering with more than 300 companies,[3] the number one success factor cited for implementing change is visible and active executive sponsorship. This factor alone is cited more frequently than any other requirement for successful implementation of business change. Employee resistance to change *increases* as the authority and sponsorship for change decreases.

Connor (*Managing at the Speed of Change*) defines sponsor as "the individual or group who has the power to sanction or legitimize change."[4] Lack of a strong executive or senior sponsor is a good predictor for failure or difficulty during change projects. Moreover, the credibility of the leading sponsor for change will be judged by employees. Some employees will distrust the change sponsor even if that sponsor holds a senior position if:

- They see frequent examples of incompetence by that sponsor

- They know of a history of failed changes

As a change leader, you need to be aware that effective sponsorship at the right level may determine success or failure of the project. Second, the sponsor's role does not decline over time. When asked about the greatest mistakes executive sponsors make, research participants[5] cited:

- Walking away from the project too soon or shifting priorities midstream

- Not being active and visible throughout the project

Executive sponsors must recognize that they are ultimately accountable for the success of the change. However, change management practitioners or consultants must coach these business leaders. Part of this role as coach is making sponsors and managers aware of the critical nature of their involvement at each phase of the project and providing them with the guidelines and tools to be successful.

An executive sponsor has three key audiences: peers, mid-level managers and employees. From the perspective of their peers, the executive sponsor has the responsibility to create a positive background conversation about the change and to build a support system. As a group, the primary sponsor, executive-level peers and key stakeholders will play one of the most important change management roles and will enable the project to be a success. Kotter (*Leading Change*) refers to this support structure for change as the "guiding coalition."[6]

From the perspective of mid-level managers, the executive sponsor has the responsibility to provide information about the change and to communicate their expectations of mid-level managers and supervisors in terms of supporting the change. The executive sponsor also has the responsibility to manage resistance from senior and mid-level managers.

From the perspective of employees, the executive

sponsor is a preferred sender of change messages. The sponsor plays a key role in communicating the business reasons for the change and the future vision for the organization.

A common mistake made by inexperienced project managers is not assessing if the change has sufficient sponsorship to succeed. Two possibilities for failure include:

- Having the right level of sponsor (e.g., CEO, senior executive), but this manager lacks the knowledge, skills and ability to act as an effective sponsor

- Not having the right sponsors at the appropriate levels throughout the organization

Moving forward with a project without creating the necessary support structure and sponsorship model will likely result in wasted resources, project delays and/or failure during implementation.

Principle 4 - Value systems

In the best-selling book *Stewardship,*[7] Block describes the values that have been the centerpiece of traditional, hierarchical organizations: control, consistency and predictability. These organizational values dictate that decision-making is at the top, leaving the execution and implementation to the middle and bottom layers of an organization.

The belief system in this type of organization is more akin to a military structure. The predictable and desired reaction to a change is compliance to any new direction, and this behavior is encouraged and rewarded. As a leader in this type of organization, authority is typically not questioned. The value systems reinforce compliant behavior, and employees understand how they will be rewarded or punished.

The values of control, consistency and predictability create an environment where change is simply a plan to implement or an adjustment to a mechanical system. Decision making is at the top. Unfortunately, as Block clearly presents, many employees are unable to serve in the best interest of the customer in this value system because they lack ownership and accountability. They do not have decision making authority nor the required business knowledge.

In this value system, the good news is that top-down change is easier to implement. The bad news is that employees are not empowered to make the right decisions at the right time to benefit the customer and the business.

Between 1960 and 2000 value systems began to shift. Business improvement initiatives that empowered employees – including Edward Deming's teachings following World-War II, the earliest quality circles from Toyota, Six Sigma from Motorola, Organization Development, Total Quality Management (TQM) from AT&T and Ford – came to the forefront. During this period, many businesses embraced one or more of these business improvement methods and the associated belief system. Over the course of implementing these improvement strategies, new values were imparted to employees including empowerment, accountability and continuous improvement (looking for ways to improve everything you do, everyday).

A new culture evolved in many of today's businesses.

Employees began to:

- Take ownership and responsibility for their work

- Have pride in workmanship and look to improve their work processes

- Feel empowered to make decisions that improve their product and the level of customer service

- Focus on results

These new values have improved business productivity and the ability to react to customer needs. However, the evolution from the traditional values of control, pre-dictability and consistency – values that made change relatively simple to implement – to the new values focused on accountability, ownership and empowerment has made the implementation of top-down business change more difficult. Employees in many companies have been taught to be responsive to customers and be accountable for business results.

The net result is that these same employees now question and resist new change initiatives. The response of the employee has shifted from "yes, sir" to "why are we doing that" – and business leaders must adapt (see Figure 3). A CEO or manager in the old value structure only had to issue the decree for change and expected it to happen. But when a CEO or manager tries this same approach today, employees respond by asking:

- *"Why?"*

- *"How does it impact me?"*

	Old Values	New Values
Command	"Jump"	"Jump"
Response	"How high?"	"Why?"

Figure 3 - A contrast in values

- *"If it isn't broken, why are you trying to fix it?"*

Business leaders and project managers must consider the impact of this shift in values on their ability to manage change and their role and responsibilities in the process. If your employees have embraced some or all of these new values, change management is not an option for successful change, it is a requirement.

The net effect of the value shift is that change management is needed more today than ever before because of the new value system of the workforce. Moreover, change management as a discipline must address both the organization as a whole and the individual. As a change agent or project leader, it is no longer sufficient to address only organizational change management activities, such as communication and training. Individual change management models are necessary to support employees who hold the new values of empowerment, accountability and ownership of day-to-day work.

Principle 5 - Incremental versus radical change

Change management activities should be scaled based on the type and size of the change. Change can be broken down into two types as shown in Figure 4.

Type 1 – Incremental change: In this change environment, a change will take place over a long period of time. The objectives of the change are small and deliberate improvements to a proven and successful business process. These types of changes are not normally driven by financial crisis or immediate demand for improvement, but rather a general focus on improving key business areas and specific operations over time. Examples of programs that result in incremental improvement include Six Sigma or continuous quality improvement methods such as TQM.

Type 2 – Radical change: In this environment, immediate and dramatic change is required over a short time period. Often driven by a crisis or significant opportunity facing the business, these changes are intended to produce dramatic performance improvements in business processes that are broken or no longer applicable to the current business conditions. The business change is often not an improvement on today's processes, but rather a replacement of the processes with something brand new. Example initiatives that create radical change include business process reengineering, regulatory changes, mergers and acquisitions.

With radical and dramatic change, change management is a critical success factor. With gradual or incremental change, employees have more time to adjust to the

Incremental
Improvement
(TQM, Six Sigma)

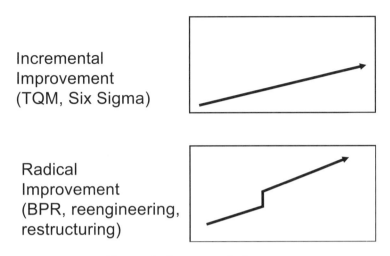

Radical
Improvement
(BPR, reengineering,
restructuring)

Figure 4 - Degrees of change

change. Change management is still required, but the scale of the change management activities will be different.

Within both types of change, you can have small and large changes. The change may impact a single work group or the entire company. The size and type of the change will affect how you, as a change leader, must scale and adjust your change management process to fit the situation.

Change management processes are most effective when they are flexible and can be scaled to fit the particular business need. No two changes will require exactly the same process or same level of change management. Even the activities and roles will change. Applying a "one-size-fits-all" approach is simply not appropriate. Scaling your change management approach will be one of the key activities you will perform when you apply change management to a new project.

Principle 6 - The right answer is not enough

A common pitfall among business managers is the assumption that the correct or "right" answer to a business problem is sufficient to overcome employee resistance. In fact, a good solution design does not mean that implementation will always be successful or that you will actually realize the business results you expect.

The error that can occur in this situation is forcing solutions onto employees because of the belief that "we know what is best." Unfortunately for managers who take this approach, employee resistance may actually increase and their changes may be unsuccessful. Even the best solutions still require change management to be effective, and you cannot assume that employees will buy-in simply because "it is the right thing to do."

Case Study 3 - The Perfect Budget

The national manager of AT&T's Services Division sequestered his staff each year for a special session. This meeting was typically held at an off-site location where the managers would be forced to maintain focus on the job at hand. That job was the annual budget. Each year they would struggle with every line item, making compromises and adjustments in the evening over dinner and then going at it again the next day until all the budget issues were resolved. Each manager would take a little and give a little, and eventually they would walk away with a budget that each manager could support.

The national manager would often disappear for long periods of time during these meetings. He viewed his role as the stage-setter, not the decision maker or the tiebreaker. Through this process he built more than just a great budget. He built a management team that could make course corrections mid-year and work together to achieve and even surpass the business objectives.

During his last year with the company, the national manager was faced with extreme budget pressure. He decided that the off-site meeting was a luxury not to be afforded in this year's budget. He cancelled the meeting for that year. Instead, he hired an outside budget consultant to work with him for several weeks to prepare the budget for each department. He was extremely proud of the detail and completeness of his work.

When the final budget was distributed to the management team, several managers approached him directly and said:

"If this is what you want, then this is what you will get."

Under other circumstances this might appear to be a statement of support. From the tone of voice used, the national manager knew differently. This was a red flag and a clear statement from his staff that he had lost their support and their trust.

During that final year the management team followed the budgets as designed, but the valuable "give and take" that used to happen throughout the year was lost. The national manager experienced more difficulties and struggles that year than any year before. The productive and dynamic interaction of this management team could not be replaced by the "perfect" budget.

Having the "right" answer can lead managers to believe that change management is not necessary. The assumption is that "if I have the right answer, employees will surely support it." Moreover, the better the solution in the mind of some managers, the harder they will fight to push that solution onto employees at any cost. In Case Study 3, allowing the managers to contribute to the budget process may not have changed the actual numbers, but it would have resulted in business managers that both understood the budget and worked together to achieve their goals even if it meant sacrifices during the year.

In large-scale changes, the feasibility of involving large numbers of employees in the design process is low. In these situations, alternate processes for involving employees must be considered as shown in Case Study 4.

Case Study 4 - The Million Dollar Barbecue

A customer service center for a large communications company needed to overhaul their processes and systems to reduce expenses. Their budget was increasing 14% year over year and was soon expected to surpass $100 million. Over 1500 employees would be impacted by the changes along with many other downstream organizations.

Representatives from every area, including more than 70 employees, comprised the project team. Design input from each department was gathered from an additional 200 employees. Even with this amount of representation, most of the 1500 people did not provide input to the solution. The project team was struggling to find ways to include more and more of the organization. Finally one team member came up with the idea that would bring everyone together for an afternoon of fun, food and money.

Since the project's main goal was to cut costs, the team decided to show a fraction of that benefit in real terms. They contracted with a local bank and treasury group to display one million dollars in cash in the main courtyard of the customer care center. Since very few people have seen one million dollars in person, this certainly got the attention of the employees. The local police helped with security, even to the point of posting officers along the main interstate highway near the buildings to prevent a robbery.

The project team combined this display of the monetary benefits from the change with a barbecue and presentations about the project including why the changes were being made and what the future state would look like. The project team was present to talk with employees and each employee could provide input and make suggestions for improvements to the design.

The combination of one million dollars, balloons, good food and access to the project team created a positive environment for change. For these employees, it was not just about how good the design was. Having the opportunity to be heard and provide input, as well as to celebrate the success, was a turning point in support of the project.

Ultimately, it is the employees who will use the new processes, tools and systems. If they understand and are supportive of the desired outcomes, then the "how" becomes less important and achieving the business objectives becomes the primary goal.

On the other hand, if project teams are determined to *force* the "right answer" onto employees, they risk employees disengaging from the process and not achieving the business objectives. Resistance to the change will likely increase. This is especially true given the previous discussion on value systems and employee ownership of their work. Effective change management programs will engage employees early in the process, focus on results and effectively integrate employee feedback into the business solution.

Principle 7 - Change is a process

The concept of change as a process has been well documented in change management literature for many years, including early work by Bridges (*Transitions*)[8] and by Beckhard and Harris (*Organizational Transitions*).[9] By breaking change down into discrete time periods or phases, change leaders can adapt their strategies and techniques based on the unique attributes of that phase (see Figure 5).

The most common lesson from this model for change is that managers must avoid treating change as a single meeting or announcement. Change is not implemented in a single moment, and likewise the role of business leaders

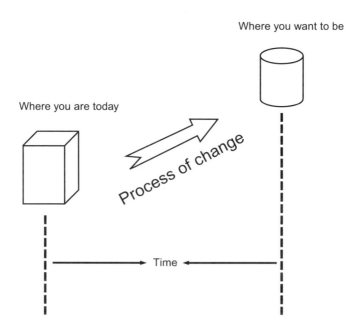

Figure 5 - The process of change

in managing change should not be reduced to a single event. The manager's role in change must be active and visible in all phases of the change process. A second practical application for this concept is to customize your change management activities according to where you are in the change process. This idea will be developed in Chapter 4.

A larger lesson from the principle of *change is a process* is found when you examine how individuals navigate change. The ADKAR change management model (*The Perfect Change*)[10], characterizes the process for individual change in five key steps:

- **Awareness** of the need to change

- **Desire** to participate and support the change

- **Knowledge** about how to change

- **Ability** to implement new skills and behaviors

- **Reinforcement** to keep the change in place

The ADKAR model captures how a single person goes through change. You can diagram this individual change process as shown in Figure 6.

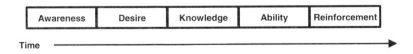

Figure 6 - ADKAR change elements

Using this model, consider that some individuals change faster or slower than others. In other words, the time it takes for each individual to go through each phase is different, and the time it takes for the entire process is also different (see Figure 7). Change management models, therefore, cannot treat the organization as a homogeneous mass of people all going through the change process at the same rate.

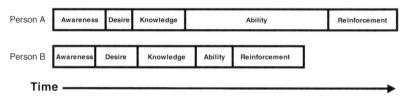

Figure 7 - Individual change progress

Now consider that each person does not find out about the change at the same time. This is especially true for large-scale changes. The resulting diagram (shown in Figure 8 for a small group of employees) illustrates the actual profile of individual change for that group.

Given this organization's ADKAR profile, you can imagine how change management processes or activities that treat the organization as a uniform group are not as effective as they could be. Individuals are going through the change at their own pace. Generic, organization-wide change management activities can miss the mark entirely by focusing energy and effort in the wrong areas at the wrong time. This is especially true for communications and training for large change projects. The result of ignoring the individual component of change is that some groups are left behind, and in many cases, the timing and content of messages is poor. Individual change management must be part of the overall program.

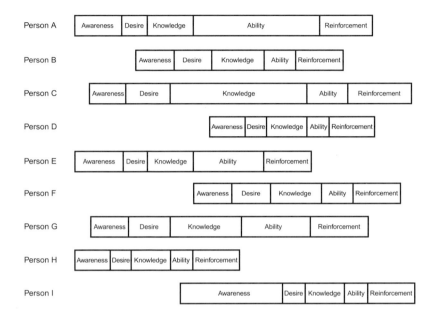

Figure 8 - Organizational ADKAR profile

Speed of the change process

A final observation for the principle that *change is a process* is to match the speed that employees navigate the change process to the speed of the business change. Figure 9 illustrates these two processes. On the vertical-axis of the figure, the standard phases of a business change are listed. On the horizontal-axis, the standard phases of personal change are shown. Successful change is defined at the upper right hand corner of this model. At this point, the business change has been fully implemented and employees have the desire, knowledge and ability to implement those changes.

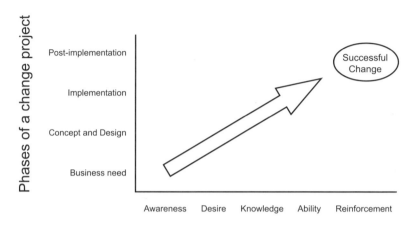

Phases of change for employees

Figure 9 - Alignment of ADKAR with business change

Common failure points for change are shown in Figure 10. Failure A occurs when more attention is paid to the business change and little or no attention is paid to the employees who are affected by the change. The result is higher turnover, loss of valued employees, reduced productivity and delays in the project. As an example, Failure A could occur if a new software package was introduced with a 1-hour training class the same day the software was to be used. If this training event was all the change management that was conducted, employees will not likely pay attention to the training because they were not even aware a change was needed. The new software package, even though better than its predecessor in design, will be less successful because the change process for employees was ignored.

Failure B occurs when the focus on employees is so extreme that the business change is not implemented

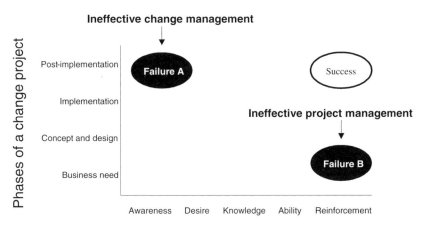

Figure 10 - Potential failure points

fully and business results are not achieved. This failure mode is possible when the resistance from employees is sufficiently great as to prevent or reduce the effectiveness of the change. An example is when a design team becomes so concerned about the needs and desires of employees, they lose sight of the business needs and what is right for the company.

Either failure point is unacceptable from a business perspective. Success is achieved when a business change is introduced and employees have the awareness and desire to implement the change, the knowledge and ability to make it happen and reinforcement to keep the change in place.

The concept of change as a process generates multiple lessons for change management teams. Managers must avoid treating changes as a single meeting or announcement. The manager's role in change must be active and visible in all phases of the change process. Finally, change management activities must be tailored according to where you are in the change.

Summary of change principles

This chapter highlighted key change principles and how they relate to managing change in the workplace. These theories and principles are essential for managing change with situational awareness and then making the necessary adjustments including scaling or modifying the change management process. Understanding and applying these principles will help you correctly apply the techniques and processes for individual and organizational change management. In summary the key concepts are:

1. Change agents must be conscious of both a sender's meaning and a receiver's interpretation.

2. Employee resistance is the norm, not the exception. Expect some employees to never support the change.

3. Visible and active sponsorship is not only desirable but necessary for success.

4. Value systems and the culture of the organization have a direct impact on how employees react to change.

5. The size and type of the change determines how much and what kind of change management is needed. Just because a change is small does not mean that change management is not required.

6. The "right" answer is not enough to successfully implement change.

7. Employees go through the change process in stages and go through these stages as individuals.

To put these principles into practice, two change management approaches are necessary as introduced in Chapter 1: the employees' perspective and the managers' perspective. Managing change from the employees' perspective is called individual change management. Managing change from the managers' perspective is called organizational change management.

Individual change management is often overlooked by many change management models. Individual change management includes the tools and processes that supervisors use with their employees to manage individual transitions through change. This employee-oriented component of change management is the critical ingredient that allows a project team to:

1. Help employees through the change process

2. Create a feedback loop to business leaders and identify points of resistance

3. Diagnose gaps in communications and training

4. Implement corrective action

The most powerful change management strategies combine organizational change management techniques with individual change management tools to create a robust, closed-loop process. Chapter 3 introduces the process and tools for individual change management. Chapter 4 integrates these tools with organizational change management techniques resulting in an overall process for managing change.

References

1. Prosci. (2003). *Best Practices in Change Management.* Loveland, CO: Learning Center Publications.

2. LaMarsh, J. (1995). *Changing the Way We Change.* Reading, MA: Addison-Wesley, p 46.

3. Prosci. (2002). *Best Practices in Business Process Reengineering Benchmarking Report.* Loveland, CO: Learning Center Publications.

4. Conner, D. (1993). *Managing at the Speed of Change.* New York: Villard Books, p 106.

5. Prosci. (2003). *Best Practices in Change Management.* Loveland, CO: Learning Center Publications.

6. Kotter, J. (1996). *Leading Change.* Boston: Harvard Business School Press, p 6.

7. Block, P. (1993). *Stewardship.* San Francisco: Berrett-Koehler Publishers.

8. Bridges, W. (1980). *Transitions* (2nd ed.). New York: Perseus Publishing.

9. Beckhard, R., & Harris, R. (1977). *Organizational Transitions.* Reading, MA: Addison-Wesley.

10. Prosci. (1998). *The Perfect Change.* Loveland, CO: Learning Center Publications.

CHAPTER 3

Individual change management

Individual change management is the process of providing tools and training to employees to enable them to manage their personal transition through change. This includes training for managers and supervisors to equip them with the tools they need to assist their employees through the change process.

This chapter shows how the ADKAR model can be used as an individual change management tool. You will have the opportunity to create an ADKAR profile for someone close to you and find out how a graduating daughter unlocked the door to change for her father.

The chapter will be dedicated to four change management objectives that can be achieved using this individual change management approach:

- **Manage personal transitions**. Individuals can assess where they are in the change process and identify their own personal barriers to change.

- **Focus conversations**. Communications with employees can be targeted to where they are in the change process, thereby enabling productive and focused conversations centered on their area of interest or conflict.

- **Diagnose gaps**. Collective input from employees provides a diagnosis of why a change may be failing or is not as effective as planned.

- **Identify corrective actions**. A framework can be created to identify corrective actions during the change process.

Using ADKAR for individual change management

The ADKAR model (*The Perfect Change*)[1] presents five stages that individuals go through when making a change:

- **Awareness** of the need to change

- **Desire** to participate and support the change

- **Knowledge** about how to change

- **Ability** to implement new skills and behaviors

- **Reinforcement** to keep the change in place

This model identifies both the stages and sequence required for an individual to experience successful change. In the following pages we provide both an exercise and a case study to illustrate this model. In teaching this approach, we have found that this exercise is the fastest way to become familiar with the ADKAR model.

Exercise

Begin by identifying a change in behavior you would like to see happen with a friend, family member or work associate. Using the worksheets in Appendix B, rate each area on a scale of 1 to 5. A score of "1" means that you are giving this area the lowest score (e.g., a score of 1 for awareness means that you believe the person is completely unaware of the reasons a change is needed). A score of "5" indicates the highest degree of compliance or understanding for that area. Be sure you select a behavior change you have been trying to support in a friend, colleague or family member that *is not working*. The worksheets in Appendix B include the following activities:

Briefly describe the personal change in behavior you are trying to facilitate with a friend, family member or work associate:

1. **Awareness**. List the reasons you believe the change is necessary. Review these reasons and rate the degree to which this person is aware of the reasons or need to change (see rating scale in Appendix B).

2. **Desire**. List the factors or consequences (good and bad) for this person that create a desire to change. Consider these motivating factors, including the person's conviction in these factors and the associated consequences. Rate his/her desire to change.

3. **Knowledge**. List the skills and knowledge needed to support the change, including if the person has a clear picture of what the change looks like. Rate this person's knowledge or level of training in these areas.

4. **Ability**. Considering the skills and knowledge needed to change, evaluate the person's ability to perform these skills or act on this knowledge. Rate this person's ability to implement the new skills, knowledge and behaviors to support the change. Are there any barriers preventing this person from acting?

5. **Reinforcement**. List the reinforcements that will help to retain the change. Are incentives in place to reinforce the change and make it stick? Rate how well the reinforcements help support the change.

See Appendix B for complete worksheets.

Once you have completed the worksheets, consider the first area in which the score was "3" or below. This is the first area that must be addressed before anything else is done. Many people prefer to see their results in a graphical format. You can create an ADKAR profile for your results by simply making a bar graph as shown in Figure 11.

If you identified *awareness* as the area with a "3" or lower score, then working on desire, knowledge or skill development will not facilitate the change. The first step is to communicate the reasons the change is necessary. Recall the sender and receiver model from Chapter 2 when working on this step.

On the other hand, if you identified *desire* as the first stage of the model with a score of "3" or below, then continually repeating your reasons for change is not adequate to move forward and may only cause aggravation. Once a person has awareness of the need for change, you

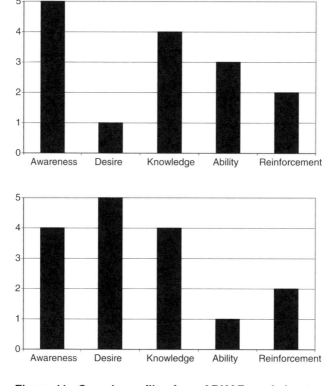

Figure 11 - Sample profiles from ADKAR worksheet

must address their inherent desire to change. Desire may stem from negative or positive consequences. The negative consequences have to be great enough to overcome their personal threshold to resist change. The same goes for positive consequences.

If *knowledge* was the area you identified, then you want to be careful not to dwell on the motivating factors. This could be discouraging for someone already at this phase. What is needed is education and training for the skills and behaviors that are required by the change.

If *ability* was the area selected with the low score, then two elements are required to move forward.

- The person will need time to develop the new skills and behaviors. Just like learning a new sport or any new skill, time is required to develop new abilities.

- The person will need ongoing coaching and support. No one-time training event or educational program will substitute for ongoing coaching and mentoring.

In certain cases, external intervention may be required to remove barriers that prevent a person from implementing the change. These barriers could be physical or psychological obstacles that require external assistance.

Finally, if *reinforcement* was the area identified, then you will need to investigate if the necessary elements are present to keep the person from reverting back to old behaviors. Address the incentives or consequences for not acting in the new way.

Case Study 5 - Scott's Junkyard

A good friend in our neighborhood has a yard full of junk.

To protect his identity, we will call him "Scott." Almost every neighborhood has one of these individuals that loves to collect anything and everything and leave it lying around. At every party, he was affectionately called "Sanford" (from the old TV show called Sanford and Son with Red Fox who ran a junk yard).

He was definitely aware that his neighbors noticed the junk, as they often asked him when that "stuff" would disappear. In the *awareness* category, he received a score of 5. On the *desire* front, Scott was hesitant to take any action. He had no compelling reasons to relocate this treasure chest of items. Going to garage sales was entertainment for Scott. He would definitely score a 1 on desire. In terms of *knowledge* and *ability*, Scott was on a first name basis with many auction companies and individuals who would happily come by and take the collection off his hands. Locating trash removal companies to cart off the remaining garbage would be easy for Scott. In both knowledge and ability, Scott would score a 5. In terms of *reinforcement*, Scott's score diminished rapidly. Whenever a neighbor was missing a "this" or a "that," they would go to Scott for help since he collected many of the common things that we all need. And then they would thank him for having the part they were looking for. Reinforcement scores a 1, thanks to the same neighbors who wanted the mess to be cleaned up. Overall Scott's scores were 5,1,5,5,1 (see Figure 12).

Since desire was the first area below a 3, that would be the area to work first. But since this was Scott's pastime, the threshold for desire was very high. It so happened that Scott had a daughter approaching high school graduation, and Scott was looking forward to the graduation party. He had great plans to have everyone over to celebrate this wonderful event and talked repeat-

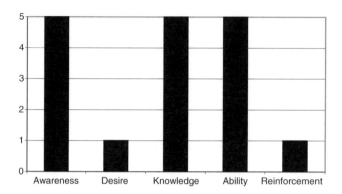

Figure 12 - ADKAR profile for Scott

edly with her about how much he looked forward to this party. As graduation approached, Scott's daughter had still not invited anyone to the party. Scott became worried. Time was running out. If she did not start sending invitations, it would be too late. Finally Scott sat down with her and asked if she was ever going to mail the invitations. With tears in her eyes, she finally told him that she would be embarrassed to have anyone over to their house for graduation because of the junk everywhere.

In a heartbeat, Scott's score for desire went from a 1 to a 5. After one week and multiple trips to the junk yard, Scott had completely cleared his yard of the years of collectibles. The party went on as planned.

For Scott, his personal obstacle to change was desire. For every person, the change barrier will be unique depending on their situation and the change itself. The purpose of the personal exercise you completed earlier in this chapter and Scott's story is to introduce the ADKAR model as a framework for looking at individual change management and how you can manage individual transitions. With this framework you can help an individual go through change. You can also use this model as a communication framework, as a diagnostic tool and as a way to identify corrective action for business changes.

ADKAR as a communication framework

Too often business leaders fall into the trap of communicating broad and general messages about change. Employees' reactions can also be generally broad. The resulting conversations are non-targeted and often unproductive. Take for example the announcement of a new software tool for customer order taking. If the change is implemented and employees believe it was not needed (i.e., they were not aware that any changes were required), then their reaction might be:

"This is a waste of time."

"Why change if it was working just fine before?"

"They never tell us what's going on!"

"Our old system was better than this one."

The natural reaction to change, even in the best circumstances, is to resist. Awareness of the business need to change is a critical ingredient of any change and must come first.

If someone had taken the time to create the initial awareness of why the change was needed, the resulting dialogue would change. In this example, if the management team had explained that the old software would no longer be supported by the vendor and that new software was necessary to meet the needs of customers, then

employee reaction, based on this awareness, would likely
be very different:

"How soon will this happen?"

"How will this impact me?"

"Will I receive new training?"

The ADKAR model provides focus for conversations about
change. It gets at the heart of the matter quickly. Using
the framework of the ADKAR model, you can clarify communications to center on the most relevant topic and
avoid unproductive conversations. Having a framework
for change helps a business leader avoid sending the
wrong messages or spending time on the wrong topics.

The stages of the model can also be used to identify
when objections to the change are actually not objections
to the design or the solution, but simply resistance to
change. When engaging in a debate with an employee
about the change, it is often difficult to distinguish legiti-
mate concerns over the new solution from simple
resistance to new ways of doing things. When this is
occurring, you can step back from the debate about the
solution and ask specific questions:

Around awareness:
   *"Do you understand and agree with the business
   reasons for making this change?"*

Around desire:
   *"Do you want this change to happen or would you
   prefer to keep things the way they are? What would
   cause you to want this change to happen?"*

Around knowledge:

"Do you know about the change and the required skills to support the change?"

Around ability:

"Are you capable of performing these new skills?"

Around reinforcement:

"Are you receiving the necessary support and reinforcement to sustain this change?"

These types of questions can isolate a potential gap or trouble-spot and change the conversation from a general complaint about the change to a targeted conversation. Approaching change without an individual change management model is like trying to describe a photograph without using shapes or colors. Without a common framework and reference point, conversations can quickly become unproductive.

As a diagnostic tool

To be effective as a change leader, you need to determine if your change management efforts are succeeding and to diagnose problem areas. If individual change management is being used concurrently with organizational change management techniques, then you can create an effective process for gathering diagnostic feedback.

Consider the ADKAR profile data that was presented for Scott in Case Study 5 or that you generated from the ADKAR exercise. Now imagine having that type of data for 10, 100 or 1000 employees. If supervisors and managers are already using individual change management tools like ADKAR with their employees, then a systematic analysis of this data is invaluable to the change management effort. From a diagnostic perspective, the change management team can identify trends and patterns from this data. It is not even necessary to have names of individual employees. Supervisors and managers can assist by simply providing general data for their groups.

Armed with this information, the change management team can diagnose the biggest gaps in their change management efforts. In some cases, these gaps may be localized to certain groups or departments. In other cases, these gaps may have resulted from mis-information or unclear messages from managers. For example, if you were working with multiple departments on a major change initiative, by collecting data from the ADKAR assessments you may discover that Department A is dealing with issues around awareness and desire, while Departments B and C are dealing with knowledge and ability issues of their employees. The net effect of this data analysis is a structured feedback or measurement process that allows you to understand and identify gaps in the change management process.

As a corrective action tool

After collecting feedback on change management activities, finding the root cause for employee resistance is the first step to identifying corrective action. The stages of the ADKAR model provide a high-level framework for categorizing feedback from employees and understanding the source of resistance. We recommend this framework because it is oriented toward the employee, and therefore the resulting corrective action is targeted at the transition stages for employees. This is a much different approach than categorizing feedback based on an organizational change management framework. In an organizational change management framework, you would likely select categories for organizing feedback like:

- Communications

- Training

- Sponsor activities

- Rewards

Unfortunately, this is structuring feedback around activities and not results. For example, saying that you need better or more communications does not accurately describe what types of communications are needed. If you use an individual change management model, the categories for organizing feedback would be:

- Awareness

- Desire

- Knowledge

- Ability

- Reinforcement

This results-oriented framework will provide the necessary direction for creating corrective action plans and activities. For example, if you determine that a major gap is knowledge about the change itself and the required new skills, then you can develop the appropriate communication and training plans to correct this knowledge gap. Project teams that can maintain a results-orientation are in a better position to develop and implement corrective action based on the root cause of employee resistance.

Individual change management summary

This chapter introduced the ADKAR model of individual change management and how it can be used in an organization. Individual change management is valuable to:

- Manage personal transitions and as a coaching tool for managers to use with their employees

- Focus conversations, especially when dealing with resistant employees

- Diagnose gaps in the change management program for each group or department

- Identify corrective action based on specific desired results

The process for using individual change management tools like ADKAR begins with training for managers and supervisors. These front-line coaches are a critical component of individual change management. In many cases, these managers and supervisors will be the "trainers" for their groups when it is not feasible for your company to train every employee about change management.

The central activities of individual change management are assessments and individual coaching. Both the employees and the supervisors need to be aware of their role and how to participate in individual change management. Worksheets for a business change, like those provided in Appendix B, are key components of this assessment and coaching process.

The final activities in individual change management include data collection, root cause analysis and corrective action based on this data. Through this process the change management team can determine what is working and what is not, and take the necessary steps. This feedback process is the integration point between individual change management and organizational change management, as presented in Chapter 4.

Getting started

The first step to applying individual change management with employees is to provide supervisors and managers with training and tools. This training will provide a solid understanding of the activities and worksheets that should be used in team meetings and individual coaching sessions.

ADKAR training, worksheets and guidelines for applying individual change management with employees are available at the Change Management Learning Center at www.change-management.com. Specifically for managers, a resource called the *"Change Management Guide for Managers and Supervisors"* is available that details how the ADKAR model is used with their teams. See Appendix A for more details.

References

1. Prosci. (1998). *The Perfect Change*. Loveland, CO: Learning
    Center Publications.

CHAPTER 4

Organizational change management

Businesses tend to have more managers who believe they have the right answers to business problems than managers who can effectively implement good ideas. As a leadership competency, change management is often lacking. The political environment combined with employee resistance stops many managers from being true leaders of change.

In this chapter we provide an overview of a comprehensive, research-based change management process that can be a starting point for developing this competency. We will discuss how individual change management tools and organization-wide techniques can be combined to effectively manage change. The Stripes and Tar case study from Chapter 1 will be continued and we will show how damage control can become the focus when change management is started too late.

Based on Prosci's research in change management over the course of three separate studies with more than 500 organizations, the most effective change management process consists of three phases including:

Phase 1 - Preparing for change

Phase 2 - Managing change

Phase 3 - Reinforcing change

This chapter provides an introduction to this process as shown in Figure 13 and summarizes the key steps. Phase 1 can be considered a time for contemplating your strategy. Phase 2 is the time for planning and action. Phase 3 is the time for reinforcing and celebrating success.

Preparing for change (Phase 1) includes activities to prepare yourself and your team for managing the change, to prepare business leaders to support the change and to create a high-level change management strategy. This first phase of change management activities can be considered a "getting ready" period. During this phase, you will:

- Assess the scope of the change, including:
  How big is this change? How many people are affected? Is it a gradual or radical change?

- Assess the readiness of the organization impacted by the change, including: *What is the value-system and background of the impacted groups? How much change is already going on? What type of resistance can be expected?*

- Acquire project resources and assess the strengths of your change management team.

- Assess the change sponsors and take the first steps to enable them to effectively lead the change process.

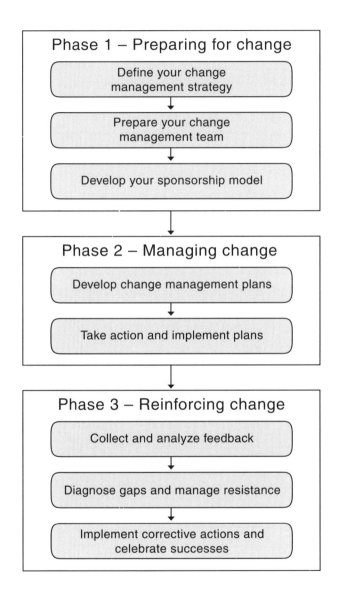

Figure 13 - Change management process

Your change management strategy is a direct result of these assessments and the degree of risk you face. For example, a large, radical change made to a large, "change-resistant" organization will entail more project risk and require more change management. Conversely, a small change made to a single department or group will require less change management and fewer activities (see Figure 14). The initial assessment tells you the depth and breadth of the change management effort.

Given this initial assessment, you can make fundamental strategy decisions related to the project. These decisions will impact your change management team structure and sponsorship model. In addition, the assessments of the size of the change and the organizational attributes will guide decision-making during the planning process for communications, training, coaching and sponsor activities. This scaling effort is what makes change management effective.

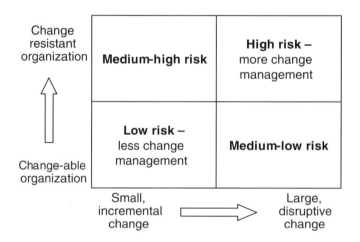

Figure 14 - Change management scaling

Once the change management strategy is set, you can select and prepare a change management team. These team members are selected and trained prior to creating detailed change management plans. Depending on the outcome of the initial assessments, the change management team may be as small as one part-time person (yourself) or as large as a core team with several sub-teams.

Concurrent with preparing the change management team, a sponsorship model is selected. A sponsorship model is the desired support structure of business leaders necessary to charter, authorize and lead the change. Sponsorship models could be as large as a steering committee of key executives or as small as one project champion working with the project team. This decision is based on the size of the change and the nature of the organization that is changing.

Along with the selection of a sponsorship model, your business leaders and stakeholders (any individual or group who has processes, systems or people affected by the change) are evaluated based on their support or opposition to the change. This assessment provides you with a benchmark of *who's who* and *where do they stand*. This is the starting point for building sponsorship for the change throughout the organization.

Think of this preparation phase like getting ready for a trip. When making plans for a major world-wide excursion you may ask questions like: "where are we going to travel," "how hard is it to get there," "will we need special assistance or guides," and "what visas and documents are required." These questions and the evaluation of the answers will help your trip go smoothly. Now consider an evening trip to a local sporting event. Not only are the answers to these questions different, even the questions will change. You will scale your trip plans accordingly. Likewise, change management requires you to scale your activities. By asking questions about the change and the impacted organization, you can choose the best change management approach and team structure to fit that situation.

In the most straight-forward terms, a good change leader will look at the change, their team and their sponsors and ask the question, "do I have the right ingredients to succeed?" If no, then you need to adjust your team, enhance your sponsorship, or scale back the change. The goal is to match the degree of sponsorship with the scope of the change.

Phase 2 - Managing change includes the design of the organizational change management plans and individual change management activities. This second phase of change management involves the planning and implementation of:

- Communication plans

- Coaching plans

- Training plans

- Sponsor roadmaps

- Resistance management plans

Communication plan - Many managers assume that if they communicate clearly with their employees, their job is done. Recall from Chapter 2 and the principles of change that there are many reasons why employees may not hear or understand what their managers are saying. You may have heard that messages need to be repeated 6 to 7 times before they are cemented into the minds of employees. That is because each employee's readiness to hear depends on the many factors discussed in Chapter 2. Effective communicators carefully consider three components: the audience, what is said and when it is said.

For example, the first step in managing change is building awareness around the need for change and creating a desire among employees. Therefore, the initial communications should be designed to create awareness around the business reasons for change and the risk of not changing. These early communications should not be cluttered with details that will distract from the key messages. Likewise, at each step in the process, communications should be designed to share the right messages at the right time.

Communication planning, therefore, begins with a careful analysis of the audiences, key messages and the timing for those messages. The change management team must design a communication plan that addresses the needs of front-line employees, supervisors and executives. Each audience has particular needs for information based on their role in the implementation of the change. As a starting point, the following communication checklist taken from the *Change Management Toolkit* (Prosci)[1] provides a summary of the most important communication topics for managing change.

Messages about the business today (shared during the earliest stages of the change)

- The current situation and the rationale for the change

- The business issues or drivers that created a need for change
- Competitive issues or changes in the marketplace including customer issues
- Financial issues or trends
- What might happen if a change is not made (the risk of not making the change)

Messages about the change (shared after employees under-stand the business situation and business reasons for change)

- A vision of the organization after the change takes place
- Scope of the change (including process scope, organizational scope, systems and technology scope)
- Objectives for the change, including a definition of success
- Alignment of the change with the business strategy
- How big of a change is needed (how big is the gap between today and the future state)
- Who is most impacted and who is least impacted
- The basics of what is changing, how it will change, and when it will change, including what will not change

Messages about how the change impacts employees (shared concurrently with messages about the change)

- The expectation that change will happen and is not a choice

- The impact of the change on the day-to-day activities of each employee
- WIIFM - "What's in it for me?" - from an employee's perspective
- Implications of the change on job security
- Specific behaviors and activities expected from employees
- Procedures for getting help and assistance during the change
- Ways to provide feedback

The schedule for the project overall (shared when available)

- The overall timeframe for the change
- When will new information be available
- How will information be shared about the project
- Major milestones and deliverables
- Key decision points
- Early success stories

Coaching plan - Supervisors will play a key role in the change management program. Ultimately, the direct supervisor has more influence over an employee's motivation to change than any other person at work. Unfortunately, supervisors as a group can be the most difficult to convince of the need for change and can be a source of resistance. It is vital for the change management team and executive sponsors to gain the support of supervisors and to build change leadership. Individual change management activities as discussed in Chapter 3 should be used to help these supervisors through the change process.

Once managers and supervisors are on board, the change management team must prepare a coaching strategy. They will need to provide training for supervisors including how to use individual change management tools with their employees.

Training plan - Training is the cornerstone for building knowledge about the change and the required skills. Project team members will develop training requirements based on the skills, knowledge and behaviors necessary to implement the change. These training requirements will be the starting point for the training group or the project team to develop training programs.

Sponsor roadmap - Business leaders and executives play a critical sponsor role in change management. The change management team must develop a plan for sponsor activities and help key business leaders carry out these plans.

Sponsorship should be viewed as the most important success factor. Avoid confusing the notion of sponsorship with support. The CEO of the company may support your project, but that is not the same as sponsoring your initiative. Sponsorship involves active and visible participation by senior business leaders throughout the process. Unfortunately many executives do not know what this sponsorship looks like. Your role includes helping senior executives do the right things to sponsor the project. Details on preparing sponsor plans and communications for executives can be found in the *Change Management Toolkit* (see Appendix A for more information).

Resistance management plan - Resistance from employees and managers is normal. Persistent resistance, however, can threaten a project. The change management team needs to identify, understand and manage resistance throughout the organization using the techniques outlined in Chapter 3 for individual change management.

Each of these plans and activities must be customized based on your change and the unique attributes of your organization. The goal of each of these plans is to support employees through the transition.

Once the change management team has completed the planning process, implementation begins. In reality, it is never as clean as Step A, Step B, Step C and so on. Most teams are implementing some plans while creating and adjusting others. If you are starting change management in the middle of a project, you could be implementing some activities before the plans are even finalized. The fact is that projects move forward with or without you. Messages are being sent every day that may help or hurt the change. Key stakeholders throughout the organization will continue to communicate with their employees whether or not the change management team is ready.

In the trip analogy, the *managing change* phase is equivalent to creating detailed checklists, packing up and heading out. You will need to determine the how, when and who of each aspect of your journey. The more complex the trip, the more detail and care you will take in this stage. Checklists become critical to ensure that key items like tickets and passports are not forgotten. At some point, you depart. This is when your plans turn into reality and the trip begins. In the *managing change* phase, you will create change management plans and implement those plans for your project.

However, we all know that not every aspect of a trip goes as planned. Unexpected events including the weather, car trouble, cancelled flights or congested highways can result in the need for course corrections. In these situations we review the plans, make alternate arrangements and continue onward. For change management, this is the role of Phase 3.

In *Phase 3 - Reinforcing change*, you will assess the results of the change management activities and implement corrective action. This phase also includes celebrating early successes, conducting "after-action reviews" and transferring ownership of the change from the change management team to the organization.

This reinforcement phase begins with an assessment of the results of the change management activities by collecting feedback from employees. The data collection process also includes compliance audits to determine if the new processes and tools are being used properly. For simple changes, this process is as straight-forward as listening and watching. These assessment results form the basis for corrective action plans and resistance management activities. The change management team analyzes the results of the feedback and compliance audits, determines the root cause of key problems and creates plans to correct these problems.

Celebrating successes, especially early wins for the project, is a critical component of change management. The change management team, however, must actively seek out these early successes and arrange for the recognition of these events. Too often, projects overlook the importance of celebrating achievements with employees. Case Study 4 demonstrates how a celebration (and one million dollars in cash) impacted employee support and further engaged them in the implementation.

The transition of the overall change process to the

operational managers of the organization enables the managers running the day-to-day operation to take control. They will assume the role of reinforcing the change and rewarding ongoing performance.

The final step in the change management process is the after-action review. It is at this point that you can stand back from the entire program, evaluate successes and failures, and identify process changes for the next project. This is part of the ongoing, continuous improvement of change management for your organization and ultimately leads to change competency.

One of the biggest mistakes many change management teams make is not completing this third phase of reinforcing change. In some cases, change management activities are stopped after initial communications and training activities are finished. This approach does not complete the process of change management and can ultimately result in the same types of failure that come from no change management at all.

Case Study 2 - Stripes and Tar continued

In the first part of this case study from Chapter 1, the president of a business association failed to implement a simple maintenance project because of resistance from business owners. Three months later a new board of directors was elected. Still on the docket, the parking lot project was the first task at hand for the new board. They began by assessing the relative complexity of this project and potential resistance from owners. Although a simple change, the board recognized that some business owners may resist this project for financial reasons. They decided that the best strategy for this change was a mail campaign along with one-on-one meetings with potentially resistant owners. A meeting of the entire association would not be required. They put together plans for a 6-week advance notification letter to each owner, followed by a reminder two weeks before construction was to begin. Seven days before work started, a final notice would be provided along with barricades that would be noticeable but out of the way until the day of the project.

The board created a communications plan including the content for each mailing. Key questions were answered in each letter, including why the change was needed, what was the risk of not implementing this change and when the change would occur. The letters also addressed how long-term maintenance costs would be lower if the change was made, resulting in lower fees to the business owners.

The new board implemented the change management plan. The notices went out on time with carefully framed messages in each communication. The barricades showed up seven days before the work began – a very visual way to remind business owners, employees and customers that change was coming soon. The board also talked with selected owners to address potential areas of resistance and to ensure that the message they were sending was being understood and well-received.

Not only did the business owners not resist the change, they actually helped ensure that on the day of the project every single car was removed from the parking area. The project was implemented without a single complaint.

Although a very simple change, this case study shows how proactive change management can change a failure into a success. The board followed all three phases of change management. First, they began by assessing the change and the organization to be impacted. They chose a strategy that fit the size and complexity of the change. Second, they created a change management plan including communications to the business owners. They carefully selected the timing and key messages for each notice and implemented the plans on schedule. Finally, they talked with selected owners just before and after the project to ensure that their communications were understood and that no additional action was required.

Managing the people side of change, whether on a large company-wide consolidation project or with a very small change project, does not require difficult or complex steps. What is required is the application of a thoughtful process for managing the change that is customized for the size and complexity of each project. The three phases introduced in this chapter form the framework for this type of structured change management process.

Avoiding damage control and "fire fighting"

Following a structured process for managing change is most effective when it begins at the same time that the business change begins. However, the reality in today's environment is that change management is not always initiated at the start of a new project. Too late in many cases, managers rush to implement change management tactics only after problems surface. The result is frantic work to control the damage and to put out "fires."

Since not all projects begin using change management at the onset, you may need to adjust your approach depending on where you are in the project lifecycle. As a change management leader or consultant, you may find yourself in several entry-point scenarios.

1. The project has just started and change management will be applied from the very beginning. This typically occurs when someone from your team, your project sponsor or you brings change management to the project as a required discipline. This is the best-case scenario.

2. The project team has completed the planning and solution design activities and has decided to apply change management now that implementation is starting. Existing team structures and roles are defined and change management is being layered onto an existing process.

3. The project is well underway and implementation has already begun. The project team is already experiencing resistance to the change. Change management is a reaction to the issues created by this resistance. This is the worst-case scenario.

The importance of entry-points for change management is two-fold. First, the later in the project you begin change management activities, the more difficult the task of managing change becomes. It is easier to prevent than fix. When starting late, your initial work will most likely be damage control. Second, many change management models are prescriptive (i.e., recipe-driven). This can be a problem if your step-by-step process assumes that you are starting at the beginning, when really you are jumping in at the middle of a project. Your understanding of change management principles will be critical for success in this situation.

If you are asked to implement change management in a project that is already underway, be aware that you will need to spend considerable time evaluating what has already been communicated to employees, both directly and indirectly. You will also have to review the existing sponsorship model and training programs to determine gaps and to identify any mis-information that may have been shared about the change. An individual change management approach like ADKAR is useful for assessing and correcting these types of situations.

As an organization gains competency in managing change, the practices and techniques of change management are initiated earlier. If you are in a position to influence your business projects, the most significant recommendation you can make is to have change management be a required practice at the beginning of every new project. When change management becomes part of "business as usual" the organization begins to build change competency as described in Chapter 5.

Connecting change management and business improvement methodologies

Many processes exist for improving business performance. A common dilemma of project managers is figuring out how to connect their business improvement program with change management. Examples of business improvement programs include:

- Six Sigma

- Business Process Reengineering (BPR)

- Total Quality Management (continuous improvement)

- Restructuring or reorganization

- Organization Development (OD)

In addition, consulting firms bring their own methods and processes for diagnosing and solving business problems. All of these business improvement approaches can and should use change management. To understand how change management activities are integrated into business improvement strategies, consider the following simple models. A business improvement program can be reduced to the following generic process.

Business improvement process steps

1. Problem or opportunity identification

2. Project planning and team formation

3. Data gathering and business solution design

4. Process and system development

5. Implementation and measurement

Likewise, most change management models include some of the following elements as discussed here in Chapter 4.

Change management components

A. Organization and change assessments

B. Team readiness and sponsor preparation

C. Awareness building, communications and training

D. Coaching, feedback and employee involvement

E. Resistance management

Now consider how these change management activities interact with a business improvement program. In the best case scenario, when the starting point for change management is at the start of the project, you can embed the change management steps and activities discussed in this chapter with the business improvement steps (see Figure 15). In this model, the overall process becomes a

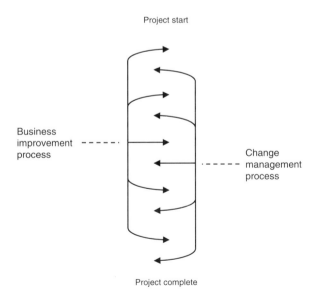

Figure 15 - Integration of change management

seamless integration of both the improvement process and the change management process.

Conversely, if change management begins later, the process is typically an overlay of change management practices on top of existing project activities. In this situation, the ability to integrate activities presents a greater challenge (see Figure 16). Resistance may already be present. Change management serves as a tool to fix the current problems and avoid similar issues in the future. Integration with the business improvement activities and team structure is difficult this late in the process.

Each scenario presents different challenges to the change management team and requires the change management process to be flexible to meet the needs of the business.

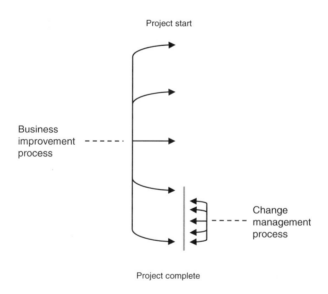

Figure 16 - Change management layering

Organizational change management summary

Organizational change management is a management responsibility. It involves using individual change management tools like ADKAR and using organization-wide tools like communications and training to realize successful change. Most importantly, organizational change management is the use of a structured change management process that helps employees through the process of change with minimal disruption to the business.

In many cases when you have been chartered with change management, the expectation may only be a few communications or perhaps a training program. Robust change management includes communication and training, but also includes the tools and processes for building effective sponsorship, enabling supervisors to lead change with their employees and managing resistance. Finally, good change management processes close the loop by listening to employees, developing corrective action programs and celebrating successes.

References

1. Prosci. (2003). *Change Management Toolkit.* Loveland, CO: Learning Center Publications.

CHAPTER 5

Change competency

Throughout this book, the term change management has been used in relation to managing change with one or more business initiatives. But what happens when change becomes the norm? Current economic conditions have placed a premium on an organization's ability to be flexible, quick to market, scalable and responsive to unique customer demands.

An organization that faces constant demands to change and uses effective change management over and over with each new initiative may experience a fundamental shift in its operations and the behavior of its employees. Sponsors begin to repeat activities that made the last change successful. Managers develop skills to support employees through the change. Employees see part of their job as navigating these new changes. Each level in the organization will have internalized its role in change and developed the skills and knowledge necessary to react to constant change. The organization has become ready and able to embrace change; it has developed change competency.

Building change competency in an organization is not like installing a new computer system or implementing a new procedure. Change competency requires a new attitude and approach. Individuals in a change-competent organization define their job in relation to change. They value the ability to change as one of their primary responsibilities. They understand that change will occur, expect it and support the change during implementation.

Change competency is the infusion of a business culture that expects change and reacts with the understanding, perspectives, tools and techniques to make change seamless and effortless. It is making change a part of "business as usual."

Change competency is similar to change management, but there are several key distinctions. First, change management is ultimately the use of specific activities (like communication, coaching, sponsorship and training) to realize successful outcomes with business changes. Change competency is not a specific activity; it is an organization's ability to react to change over and over again.

Second, while change management can be taught and learned, change competency requires a fundamental shift in culture and values. It must become part of day-to-day operations and cannot be simply demonstrated in training or instructional material.

Third, change competency must penetrate every facet and level of the organization. This distinction especially relates to the front-line employees. An organization may have expertise in change management in its sponsors, consultants and change management practitioners. However, the front-line employees are the ones whose day-to-day activities are changing. In change management, these employees are the target of much of the activity. In change-competent organizations, these employees are key participants. They must be given the perspectives, tools and techniques to rapidly and success-fully change for the organization to build change competency.

Although a main focus of organizational change man-agement, employees are often neglected when it comes to building competency in change. Training and resources are readily available for executives, change teams and even managers and supervisors. Front-line employees, however, are often left behind. Ironically, managing employee resistance is often the number one challenge for change management teams. The importance of front-line employees should not be underestimated.

Consider an employee's role in change compared to members of a project team or the executive sponsors. For the project team, the current change initiative may be the only project they work on before they move on to other opportunities in the business. The executive sponsor of the project probably has many other decisions and initia-tives to support, and this project is only a small part of the big picture. However, for the employees who must change their daily activities, this change initiative could produce dramatic and radical change to their careers. It may do away with everything they know and are comfort-able with. It may introduce systems, processes or approaches that are new and intimidating. To truly build change competency into an organization, the front-line employees must understand how they can succeed and perform in a constantly changing business world.

Evidence of a change-competent organization

Change-competent organizations, as viewed from each

role in the organization, have the following objectives:

Executive – constantly search for ways to improve profitability and growth by reacting to marketplace changes and opportunities, and ensuring that business changes are implemented and realized to their full potential through effective leadership and change sponsorship.

Project team – support sponsors, managers and front-line employees through the change process with tools, processes and techniques to manage change.

Managers – support employees through the change process; provide direction and steering for professional development and encourage successful performance in the new environment, including coaching employees on change management techniques.

Front-line employees – perform successfully in the current environment, during the transition and in the changed environment.

To build change competency, you must equip all levels of your organization with the understanding, perspectives and tools to make change seamless and effortless.

You can use the ADKAR model to assess where your organization is today relative to change competency and to develop an action plan to move in that direction. Consider and evaluate the following statements as they relate to your organization. Use the assessment process presented previously for applying the ADKAR model. If a statement accurately reflects your current state, then you would score a 5. If a statement is in strong contrast to the current state of the organization, then you would score a

1 in that area.

Awareness – the organization understands the importance of responding quickly and efficiently to internal and external pressures to change; the organization understands what change competency is and the associated business risk of not developing change competency; all groups understand the business reasons and drivers for making this shift in culture, values and skills.

Desire – all groups at all levels acknowledge that the ability to change is critical if the organization is to survive, and they are ready and willing to begin the journey toward change competency.

Knowledge – the organization has the base knowledge of what a change-able organization looks like and what skills and values are required; all facets of the organization have a basic understanding of change management theories and practices; each group understands its role in a change-competent organization.

Ability – the organization possesses and effectively utilizes the tools and processes to manage change; leaders, change practitioners and front-line employees have practice and coaching in being successful change agents and can routinely apply their knowledge and skills to realize change; barriers that prevent change implementation are readily identified and removed.

Reinforcement – the organization encourages and rewards successful change through its culture, values and initiatives; support of change competency is reinforced and resistance to change is identified and managed;

change is part of "business as usual."

Change is a process and building change competency will take time. It is important to realize that you will need to apply change management techniques to this change as well. You will need to recognize where you are today, where you want to be in the future, and what it will take to make that transition. Change management is a required capability for developing change competency.

Summary

To build change competency into your organization, you can take the first step by ensuring that solid change management practices are applied consistently for each change initiative. The second step is to begin building the following competencies into your organization. For organizational change competency, you will need to build knowledge and skills in the following areas:

- Change management planning and strategies

- Change management team structures

- Change management roles

- Organizational change management methodologies

- Executive sponsorship strategies

- Communication planning and delivery

- Training and educational programs

- Incentive and recognition programs

For individual change competency, you will need to build knowledge and skills in the following areas:

- Methods for managing employee resistance

- Models for individual change management

- Coaching tools and techniques for helping employees navigate the change process

- Activities and exercises for supervisors to use with their employees to manage change

- Incentive and recognition programs

CHAPTER 6

Conclusion

Change Management: the People Side of Change presents the foundation needed to effectively manage change. Some of you may have noticed that the book itself was organized along the ADKAR model for change.

The book began by creating **Awareness** of the need for change management and **Desire** to use change management techniques to avoid project failures or business disruptions. Change management is used for one reason – to ensure business success. Many changes do fail in organizations that do not appreciate and manage the people side of change. We presented research results that showed change management as the most critical and important activity for business improvement projects. We discussed the many forms of employee and management resistance and showed how this resistance can severely impair or stop a change project. Project teams that introduce change but do not use change management run the risk of missed project objectives, productivity losses, and sometimes complete failure.

Next, the principles and theories of change management built the necessary **Knowledge** to be an effective change agent and to scale your change management efforts. Change management does not work with a "one-size-fits-all" approach. The best and most effective change management approach will match the specific change and the particular organization that is being changed. As a practitioner, the seven principles of change are critical for understanding both why and how to use change management. The seven key principles are:

1. Change leaders must be conscious of both a sender's message and a receiver's interpretation.

2. Employee resistance is the norm, not the exception.

3. Visible and active sponsorship is not only desirable but necessary for success.

4. Value systems and the culture of the organization have a direct impact on how employees react to change.

5. The size of the change determines how much and what kind of change management is needed.

6. The "right" answer is not enough to successfully implement change.

7. Employees go through the change process in stages and go through these stages as individuals.

The chapters on individual change management and organizational change management added additional knowledge on how to manage change. In these chapters, tools and processes were introduced to increase your **Ability** to manage change. Individual change management is the process of helping individuals understand, cope with and thrive in a changing environment. As individuals, we experience change differently. We go through change in stages. We may take longer or shorter to move through each stage, and we may start at different times. For individual change management, the ADKAR model was introduced. ADKAR is a useful tool for focusing conversations about change, diagnosing the root causes of resistance, determining corrective actions and managing individual transitions.

Organizational change management is the manager's view of change – the process, activities and tools used within an organization to make a change successful. Organizational change management involves preparing for change, managing change and reinforcing change. The chapter on organizational change management presented a structured process for change management and introduced the key plans and activities that are required. It is not enough to complete an activity and move on. You must assess the impact of the activity, diagnose any gaps and develop corrective actions for organizational change management to be effective.

The mis-steps and project failures uncovered in research with other companies provide **Reinforcement** for managing the people side of change. When change management is reinforced in your company as a necessary leadership skill, the organization begins to build competencies at each level: executives, mid-level managers and front-line employees. A change-competent organization views change as part of "business as usual." Changes are not feared and resisted, but expected and embraced.

Change competency involves a shift in values, culture and operations. It is not a quick and easy competency to develop, but it is critical given the ever changing business environment.

What is the next step?

One of your key responsibilities as a manager of change is to be the champion of change management in your organization. You must demonstrate the importance of actively managing change and build support among your peers, leaders and direct reports. You must provide guidance to senior executives, managers and supervisors. You must help the organization embrace and thrive during change.

In the Appendix of this book you will find additional material to help with the processes of managing change and building change competency. In Appendix A we provide a list of change management resources to help you take the next step. In Appendix B, you will find ADKAR worksheets. In Appendix C we have included highlights from Prosci's most recent benchmarking report on change management. In Appendix D, we have listed the most commonly asked questions from employees and general answers that can serve as a starting point for your communications.

Appendices

Appendix A - Change management resources

Appendix B - ADKAR worksheets

Appendix C - Highlights of best practices

Appendix D - Frequently asked questions

Appendix A - Change management resources

Change management tutorials

You can register for free bi-weekly white papers and tutorials at www.change-management.com. Click the registration button in the menu. There is no charge for registering.

Change Management Toolkit (CD-ROM and Binder)

The <u>Change Management Toolkit</u> is a comprehensive leader's guide that contains templates and guidelines to help you effectively employ change management and write a complete and professional change management plan. Assessment tools and implementation guidelines will help you implement an effective change management strategy. The Change Management Toolkit teaches you to:

- Manage the people side of change, not just the business aspects

- Develop a change management strategy for your project

- Create a communication plan

- Actively manage resistance to change

Toolkit components:

The toolkit contains the following components:

- Change management overview - what is change management, why is it important, what can I do to manage change effectively

- Assessments - tools for evaluating your change and your organization's readiness for change

- Templates - critical document templates for planning and executing change management - provided on CD-ROM

- Theories and perspectives - a practical discussion of change principles and concepts

- Change management process - guidelines, templates and checklists for the entire change management process including planning templates for communications, training and coaching

- Customization guidelines - change management should reflect your unique change and the organization that is changing - learn how to adapt to the specifics of your project

Toolkit structure

The toolkit covers the following change management phases:

Preparing for change: Build a foundation for managing change. Examine theories and perspectives that impact how people go through change. Assess your specific change characteristics and the organizational attributes that impact change management. Develop your team structure and sponsorship model.

Managing change: Develop key change management plans: communications, sponsorship, coaching, training, and resistance management. Create a project plan for implementing change management activities and learn how to use the ADKAR model.

Reinforcing change: Assess the effectiveness of change management activities. Identify and overcome obstacles. Build buy-in and celebrate successes.

Available at www.change-management.com or by calling Prosci at 970-203-9332.

Change Management Best Practices Report (journal-style report)

The new 2003 <u>Best Practices in Change Management</u> report presents comprehensive findings from 288 companies on their experiences and lessons learned in change management. This report makes it easy to learn change management best practices and uncovers the mistakes to avoid when creating executive sponsorship. Participants share:

- How to effectively manage change

- How to combat employee resistance

- How to build executive support for your project

- What teams would do differently on their next project

Study participants include team leaders, change management advisory team members, project team members, consultants and management sponsors from 288 organizations. The report includes data from the 2003, 2001 and 1999 studies to present the most effective practices in change management.

Success factors:
Uncover the greatest contributors to the success of a change management program.

Methodology:
Learn the "must do" activities for each phase of the project: planning, design and implementation.

Role of top management:
Learn which key activities sponsors can do to contribute to the success of the project, as well as the biggest mistakes they often make.

Communications:
Determine the most effective methods of communication and find out how frequently objectives and status of the project need to be communicated.

Team structure:
Learn the top criteria for a good change management team member, and how to improve the effectiveness of your change management effort by selecting the right people.

Using consultants:
Understand the key contributions that consultants make to a project and determine how to define the consultants' roles for optimum success.

Employee's Survival Guide to Change (paperback)

"The best change management guide that a business can provide to its employees."
    Sandy D., Avaya

"A much needed addition to every employee's toolbox! The first thing to reach for when faced with change. It's like hiring a 'personal coach' at a fraction of the cost."
    Madeleine Ashe, Vanguard Communications
    Corporation

There are few tools on the market designed to help employees impacted by change. Ironically, nearly one-fourth of major change initiatives fail because employees are fearful of and resistant to change. The <u>Employee's Survival Guide to Change</u> answers questions most employees are unwilling to ask and uncovers what it takes to survive and thrive in today's changing workplace. Employees will learn the ADKAR model and how to become effective change agents instead of difficult change barriers.

The Employee's Survival Guide to Change helps you:

- Avoid the loss of valued employees and minimize business disruption caused by the change

- Answer the questions employees are afraid to ask

- Describe the phases of the change and what employees can expect

- Garner support from employees who would otherwise resist the change

- Create an attitude of "Can-do" rather than "Not my job"

Available at www.change-management.com or by calling Prosci at 970-203-9332.

Change Management Guide For Managers and Supervisors (CD-ROM and Binder)

The <u>Change Management Guide for Managers and Supervisors</u> includes detailed guidelines and exercises for managers and supervisors to assist employees through the change process. Activities and worksheets are included for working with employee groups.

Use this resource with the Employee's Survival Guide book to:

- Overcome resistance and lower employee turnover

- Avoid productivity losses caused by process, technology or organizational changes

- Lower employee stress and increase employee satisfaction

- Effectively deploy and manage change in your organization

Manager's guide structure:

Answering frequently asked questions
Paralleling the Employee's Survival Guide, the Manager's Edition provides answers and activities to address the tough questions that employees have about change.

Using the ADKAR model
This section provides a detailed description of the ADKAR model. By understanding this model, you can help your employees use this diagnostic tool to identify resistance to change and develop plans for effectively changing. This section also contains group exercises using the ADKAR model.

Managing change templates
Taking the results from the group exercises, this section

helps you build your change management strategy. This section includes the following templates:

- Business process change map

- Change management activity map

- ADKAR employee activity tracker

- Employee roadmap

- Professional development plan

Benchmarking results

This section contains the research results presented in the Employee's Survival Guide, as well as specific findings related to your role as a supervisor or sponsor of change. It details the biggest mistakes made by sponsors and the role of managers during each phase of the change process.

Available at www.change-management.com or by calling Prosci at 970-203-9332.

Additional suggested reading materials

Changing the Way We Change by J. LaMarsh (Hardcover - January 1995)

Leading Change by J. P. Kotter (Hardcover - January 1996)

Managing at the Speed of Change by D. R. Conner (Hardcover - January 1993)

Managing Transitions by W. Bridges (Paperback - May 2003 2nd edition)

Organizational Transitions by R. Beckhard and R. Harris (Paperback - 1987)

Appendix B - ADKAR worksheets

ADKAR worksheet for personal change

Briefly describe a **personal** change you are trying to support with a friend, family member or work associate.

_____

_____

_____

_____

_____

_____

_____

_____

_____

_____

_____

_____

_____

_____

_____

_____

_____

_____

_____

_____

_____

_____

_____

_____

1. List the reasons you believe the change is necessary.

_____
_____
_____
_____
_____
_____
_____
_____
_____
_____
_____
_____
_____
_____
_____
_____
_____
_____

Review these reasons and rate this person's **awareness** of these reasons for change.

Score

1	2	3	4	5
low				high

2. List the factors or consequences (good and bad) for this person that create a *desire* to change.

_____

_____

_____

_____

_____

_____

_____

_____

_____

_____

_____

_____

_____

_____

_____

Consider these motivating factors, including the person's conviction in these factors and the associated consequences. Assess his/her **desire** to change.

Score

1	2	3	4	5
low				high

3. List the skills and *knowledge* needed for the change.

_____
_____
_____
_____
_____
_____
_____
_____
_____
_____
_____
_____
_____
_____
_____
_____
_____
_____

Rate this person's **knowledge** or training in these areas.

Score

1   2   3   4   5
low   high

4. Considering the skills and knowledge identified in Step 3, evaluate the person's ability to perform these skills or act on this knowledge.

_____
_____
_____
_____
_____
_____
_____
_____
_____
_____
_____
_____
_____
_____
_____
_____

To what degree do you rate this person's **ability** to implement the new skills, knowledge and behaviors to support the change?

Score

1	2	3	4	5
low				high

5. List the *reinforcements* that will help to retain the change. Are incentives in place to reinforce the change and make it stick?

_____

_____

_____

_____

_____

_____

_____

_____

_____

_____

_____

_____

_____

_____

_____

_____

To what degree do you rate the **reinforcements** as helping support the change?

Score

1   2   3   4   5
low   high

Now transfer your scores from each worksheet to the table below. Take a moment to review your scores. Highlight the first area to score a 3 or lower. This is the starting point for managing change with this individual.

Brief description of the change:

1. **Awareness** of the need to change?

                                1   2   3   4   5

Notes:_____

2. **Desire** to make the change happen?

                                1   2   3   4   5

Notes:_____

3. **Knowledge** about how to change?

                                1   2   3   4   5

Notes:_____

4. **Ability** to change?

                                1   2   3   4   5

Notes:_____

5. **Reinforcement** to retain the change?

                                1   2   3   4   5

Notes:_____

ADKAR worksheets for business change

Briefly describe the change that is being implemented at your company.

_____

_____

_____

_____

_____

_____

_____

_____

_____

_____

_____

_____

_____

_____

_____

_____

_____

_____

_____

_____

_____

_____

_____

1. Describe your *awareness* of the need to change. What are the business, customer or competitor issues that have created a need to change?

_____

_____

_____

_____

_____

_____

_____

_____

_____

_____

_____

_____

_____

_____

_____

_____

To what degree do you rate your *awareness* of the need to change?

Score

1	2	3	4	5
low				high

2. List the factors or consequences (good and bad) related to this change that affect your *desire* to change.

_____

_____

_____

_____

_____

_____

_____

_____

_____

_____

_____

_____

_____

_____

_____

_____

_____

Consider these motivating factors, including your conviction in these factors and the associated consequences, and assess your overall desire to change.

Score

1   2   3   4   5

low   high

3. List the skills and knowledge needed to support this change.

_____

_____

_____

_____

_____

_____

_____

_____

_____

_____

_____

_____

_____

_____

_____

_____

_____

Do you have a clear understanding of the change and the skills you will need to operate in the changed environment? Have you received education or training to learn these skills? To what degree do you rate your *knowledge* of the change?

Score

1   2   3   4   5
low   high

4. Considering the skills and knowledge identified in Step 3, assess your overall proficiency in each area (low, medium, high).

_____

_____

_____

_____

_____

_____

_____

_____

_____

_____

_____

_____

_____

_____

_____

_____

Review your evaluations and rate your overall *ability* to change.

Score

1   2   3   4   5
low   high

5. List the *reinforcements* that will help retain the change.
Are incentives in place to reinforce the change and make
it stick?

_____

_____

_____

_____

_____

_____

_____

_____

_____

_____

_____

_____

_____

_____

_____

_____

To what percent do you rate the *reinforcements* as adequate to sustain the change?

Score

1   2   3   4   5
low   high

Now transfer your scores from each worksheet to the table below. Take a moment to review your scores. Highlight the first area to score a 3 or lower. This is the starting point for addressing your personal transition through this change.

Brief description of the change:

1. **Awareness** of the need to change?

                                   1 2 3 4 5

Notes:_____

2. **Desire** to make the change happen?

                                   1 2 3 4 5

Notes:_____

3. **Knowledge** about how to change?

                                   1 2 3 4 5

Notes:_____

4. **Ability** to change?

                                   1 2 3 4 5

Notes:_____

5. **Reinforcement** to retain the change?

                                   1 2 3 4 5

Notes:_____

Appendix C - Highlights of best practices

In your study of change management, listening to and learning from the experiences of others is a key step. This section provides questions and answers that will give you a head start. View these findings as if you are sitting across from a colleague from another company and asking questions like, *"what were your greatest contributors to success?"*

This chapter provides highlights of key findings from three Prosci research studies involving more than 400 companies. The following responses were synthesized from hundreds of answers to these types of questions, with the most common themes and patterns prioritized in the response. The heading of each section refers to the question answered by participants. For example, the section titled "Greatest contributors to success" provides the most common answers participants gave to the question, "What were the greatest contributors to your change management project's success?".

Greatest contributors to success

Overwhelmingly, the greatest contributor to project success was effective and strong executive sponsorship. Effective sponsors:

- Show active and visible support, both privately and professionally

- Ensure that the change remains a priority

- Demonstrate their commitment as role models of change

- Provide compelling justification for why the change is happening

- Communicate a clear understanding of the goals and objectives of the change

- Provide sufficient resources for the team and project to be successful

The top five contributors to successful change projects were:

1. Effective sponsorship (as described above)

2. Buy-in from front-line managers and employees

   Many participants highlighted the importance of support from the impacted employees and managers. Involvement early in the process increased support from these levels.

3. Exceptional team

   The change management team itself was identified as a contributor to success. The skills, expertise, experience and commitment of the team were critical. Additionally, an effective leader and motivator should lead the team.

   "The right people... highly professional, highly motivated, highly focused, highly questioning and extremely resourceful."

4. Continuous and targeted communication

Communication was identified as a key contributor to
success. Effective communication was consistent, open
and honest, targeted at the specific recipient and
delivered through a variety of media.

*"the Right communication to the Right stakeholder at
the Right time during the project."*

5. Well planned and organized approach

Organization and planning contributed to the success
of some projects, including the use of a methodology
or specific plan, initiation of change management
activities early in the project, a systematic approach to
the change and the anticipation of specific resistance.

Greatest change management obstacles

The top obstacle to change was employee resistance at all
levels. Study participants indicated that there was a natural human resistance to change that had a significant
impact on project success. The top-five greatest change
management obstacles were:

1. Employee and staff resistance

Employees were fearful of the unknown and were
opposed to moving outside of their comfort zone. The
background conversation or "coffee pot" discussions
between employees contributed to this resistance.

"Many people feel that if they wait long enough, this too shall pass."

2. Middle-management resistance

Middle managers posed a significant obstacle since they directly interact with front-line employees. Resistance was due to a perceived loss of power and/or limited input in the project.

3. Poor executive sponsorship

Executive sponsors either did not play a visible role in supporting the program or shifted their support too soon after project initiation.

"Lack of active sponsorship. We have surface 'buy-in' but lacked visible reinforcement and leadership modeling the change."

4. Limited time, budget and resources

Project teams did not have adequate time to complete the project. The strain of the change project on existing resources compounded the problem. Change projects were overshadowed by daily activities and responsibilities.

"Current resources are stretched nearly beyond capacity."

5. Corporate inertia and politics

The organizational culture pushed back against the

change initiative.

*"Unshackling the embedded culture of the organi-
zation... too many long tenured employees."*

What would you do differently on your next project?

Participants indicated that the number one thing they
would do differently in the next project was to ensure they
had sufficient support from the primary sponsor.

Responses regarding sponsor actions included the
need to:

- Clarify who is directly responsible

- Train executives and senior managers about what is
  required of an effective sponsor

  *"Articulate the specific roles, activities and behav-
  iors to the sponsor as part of their commitment to
  the initiative."*

- Illustrate the importance of change to more members
  of senior management, not just those directly involved
  with the project

- Demonstrate commitment early and maintain
  sponsor support throughout the program, not just at
  initiation

  "[Senior management should be] committed in actions,

not just words. They said that they were committed to the leadership piece, but never followed through."

The top responses for what participants would do differently next time were:

1. Ensure sponsor support.

2. Begin change management earlier in the project – not as an afterthought or add-on.

   "See change management as critical from day one, not just a nice add-on. Begin change awareness earlier."

3. Develop better and earlier communications that fully address employee concerns – answer, "What's In It For Me (WIIFM)."

   "Prepare employees for the change to eliminate psychological fear."

4. Engage users and employees earlier in the project and gather input and feedback.

5. Increase the amount of time and resources allocated for the project.

6. Form a change management team of committed top-performers with full-time dedication to the project.

Employee resistance

Participants gave a variety of reasons for resistance by employees and managers. The top-five reasons for employee resistance were lack of awareness about the change, fear of the unknown (comfort with the current state), culture, opposition to new systems or processes, and fear of job loss.

1. Lack of awareness

> Participants indicated that the primary reason for employee resistance was a lack of awareness about the change and why the change was needed. Employees did not clearly understand why the change was happening, nor did they have adequate knowledge regarding the change itself. Employees did not have the answer to the question "What's in it for me?" – or WIIFM. This could include: Will I have a job? How will it impact my daily work? How will I benefit from the change?

> Study participants stated that the most important messages to communicate to impacted employees fell into two categories: general information about the change, including why the change is needed, and information about how the change will impact them specifically. Key messages included:

> • the current situation and the rationale for the change

> • a vision of the organization after the change

- the basics of what is changing, how it will change and when it will change

- the expectation that change will happen and is not a choice

- status updates on the implementation of the change, including success stories

- the impact of the change on the day-to-day activities of the employee (WIIFM – What's in it for me?)

- implications of the change on job security (Will I have a job?)

- specific behaviors and activities expected from the employee, including support of the change

- procedures for getting help and assistance during the change

2. Comfort with the status quo and fear of the unknown

Participants indicated that employees tended to be complacent or that the current way of doing business had been in place for a long time. The current processes and systems seemed "fine" to employees, and they were opposed to the change since it forced them out of their comfort zone. Uncertainty and fear about the future state also reduced the desire of employees to change.

3. Organizational history and culture

The organization's past performance with change projects impacted the employees' perception of the current change project. Employees were desensitized to change initiatives, as many had been introduced and failed. The project was seen merely as the "flavor of the month" and employees expected it go away like those in the past.

4. Opposition to the new technologies, requirements and processes introduced by the change

Many participants felt that some employees resisted the change because of opposition to the actual change itself. Employees were opposed to changes that increased the performance requirements and measurement of their work. The change was seen as adding unwanted work, responsibility and accountability. Lastly, some employees opposed the new processes, systems or technologies because they felt the change would not solve the problems they were experiencing.

5. Fear of job loss

Employees perceived the business change as a threat to their own job security. Some employees felt that the change would eliminate the need for their job, while others were unsure of their own abilities and skills in the new environment.

Manager resistance

The top six reasons for manager resistance to change were:

1. Loss of power and control

   The leading reason for manager resistance to change was a fear of losing power. Changes often eliminated something the manager had control of, or introduced something that the manager would not have control over. Managers perceived the changes as infringements on their autonomy, and some participants indicated that the change was even perceived as a personal attack by the managers. Managers reacted to the change initiative as a "battle for turf."

2. Overload of current tasks, pressures of daily activities and limited resources

   Managers felt the change was an additional burden. Limited resources compounded the problem. The change initiative seemed like extra work and resource strain at a time when the pressures of daily activities were already high. In many projects, managers were expected to continue all of their current duties in addition to the duties of implementing the change.

3. Lack of skills and experience needed to manage the change effectively

   Managers were fearful of the new demands that would be placed on them by the business change. Several skill areas were identified as areas of concern. First, managers were uncomfortable with their role in managing the change. Some feared they would become the target of mistrust and anger from employees. Others did not have the experience or tools to effectively manage their employees' resistance. Also, managers were concerned about the skills, knowledge and responsibilities placed on them by the new business processes and technologies.

4. Fear of job loss

Managers felt that the business change would ultimately impact their own job security.

5. Disagreement with the new way

Some managers disagreed with the change. They did not feel that the solution was the best approach to fixing the problem. Managers who did not play a role or did not provide input in the design and planning phases tended to resist the solution. Some participants felt that the resistance was due to the solution not being the idea of the manager (the "not invented here" syndrome).

6. Skepticism about the need for change

Managers were not convinced of the need for change. They did not see the business issues driving the change or they did not identify the same problems as the design team.

Most common executive sponsor mistakes

Participants cited the following areas as the most common mistakes made by executive sponsors:

- Not visibly supporting the change throughout the entire process (becoming disconnected from the change)

- Abdicating responsibility or delegating down – "setting it up and leaving it to the project manager"

- Not communicating the reason and need for change and the future state (the vision) to employees and managers multiple times through multiple media

- Failing to build a coalition of business leaders and stakeholders to support the project

- Moving on to the next change before the current change is in place or changing priorities too soon after the project has started

- Underestimating resistance to change and the need to manage the people side of the change process (unwilling to deal with resistant managers or stay the course when resistance increases)

- Failing to set expectations with mid-level mangers and front-line supervisors related to the change and change process

- Spending too little time on the project to keep it on track and with the project team to help them overcome obstacles

What would project teams do differently with regard to communication?

Participants indicated that the top five changes they would make regarding their communications were:

1. More communications (more frequent)

2. Begin communications sooner in the project

3. More face-to-face communications – some participants felt that they relied too heavily on email, not recognizing the importance of a personal approach

4. More communications from executive sponsors and senior managers

5. More communications about the impact of the change on employees – answering the questions, how will this affect me and what's in it for me

About the best practices report

The highlights in this section are compiled findings from change management benchmarking studies conducted by Prosci over the past six years. For more information or to obtain copies of these reports, visit www.change-management.com.

Appendix D - Frequently asked questions

In most business changes, employees have questions that address the overall change and how they will be impacted. The answers to these questions are certainly unique to the business, the change and the employee. For example, the question *"Why is this change necessary?"* will be unique to your business conditions. However, in many cases, answers will have common themes. This chapter lists some frequently asked questions and answers taken from the book, <u>Employee's Survival Guide to Change</u> (Prosci 2002). These answers may be useful as a starting point if you are faced with similar questions.

Why is change happening now?

Most changes begin outside the company many months or even years before internal change takes place. Research shows that most major business changes are a response to changes in the external marketplace. These external marketplace changes can result in:

- New opportunities that require immediate action.

- Loss of market share (your company is losing money).

- New offers or capabilities by competitors (they're creating new business faster than your company).

- Lower prices (their cost of doing business is lower, resulting in better prices to their customers).

External business drivers take time to set in. Once they have affected the bottom line of the company, change is

needed immediately. In some cases it is already too late —
the internal change should have started much sooner.

What is the risk of not changing?

When external marketplace changes are reflected inside
the organization, managers suddenly realize the risks of
not changing.

For businesses, the risk of not changing could mean:

- Loss of jobs (even at the executive level)

- Failure in the marketplace

- Bankruptcy or loss of revenue

For employees, the risk of not changing could mean:

- Job dissatisfaction

- Fewer promotional opportunities

- Lower job security in the long term

- Immediate loss of employment

What is the rush?

We usually find out what is happening after the fact.
Organizations do not always share financial information

or talk about poor performance issues with employees. Therefore, when change is needed quickly, employees and even some managers may be taken by surprise. As a company we still need to react quickly to changing market conditions to remain viable. It may appear that the company is in a rush to change when actually it is already late in implementing change.

If I wait long enough, will the change just go away?

Waiting will usually not change the outcome of a change. In some cases, the company will change even in the face of resistance from employees, especially if financial success is at stake.

This does not imply that change will be bad for you. In the end many changes result in positive outcomes. Benefits might include better tools, improved work processes, more secure jobs and new opportunities.

What might the change mean to me?

Change to a business can include:

- New ways of doing work

- New systems or tools

- New reporting structures or job roles

- Shifting cultures or sub-cultures

- New products or services

- New markets or geographic locations

The actual change for you depends on your current job, the extent of the change, and the choices you make in response to the change.

With some changes, you may not be impacted at all. With major changes, you may be doing new work, using new tools or reporting to a new manager. With radical changes to the business, some employees may work in other departments or even move to other companies.

When the change is implemented, each person will be affected differently. In the end, how you react to the change plays an important role in how the change will impact you. In other words, what you are in control of is how you respond to change. In fact, how the organization views you and your future role in the company may depend on your response to change and the choices you make.

What are my choices?

Your choices about how to respond to change will vary as the organization moves through the change process. Think about the change in these time periods:

- When the change is first announced, but before the change is implemented.

- During the change process, when the new solution is being deployed.

- After the change is in place, following the implementation of the solution.

Your choices and their consequences depend on which phase your organization is in. The following pages provide potential choices you may make and the likely outcome of those choices. In some cases choices you make may have negative outcomes. They may be bad for you and for the organization. Other choices you make will benefit you and enhance your ability to thrive in a changing organization.

The choices shown on the following pages are separated into:

- Choices with typically *negative* outcomes

- Choices with typically *positive* outcomes

These examples help illustrate the conscious and unconscious decisions we all make regarding change.

Choices when the change is first announced

Choices that typically have a *negative* outcome when the change is first announced:

- Talk badly about the proposed change with your peers or subordinates

- Talk negatively about the organization or people in the organization

- Talk one way in public, but say otherwise in private conversations

- Stop performing your current tasks or perform them carelessly

- Have secret meetings with your subordinates where the change is minimized or not taken seriously

Choices that typically have a *positive* outcome when the change is first announced:

- Learn about the change

- Ask how you can help

- Find out how you can prepare for the change

- Display a positive outlook

- Encourage constructive conversations with fellow employees

- Be open and honest with your feedback about the change

- Be quiet and curious (this choice is acceptable during the early phases of a change)

Choices during the change transition

Choices that typically have a *negative* outcome during the transition to the new solution:

- Block progress or sabotage the change process

- Talk negatively about the change in private conversations

- Ignore the change, pretend that it is not happening (denial)

- Prevent others from participating in the design of the solution or implementation of the design

Choices that typically have a *positive* outcome during the transition to the new solution:

- Ask questions about the future

- Ask how the change will impact day-to-day operations

- Provide input to the solution

- Find out what new skills and abilities you will need to perform effectively after the change is in place

- Assess your own strengths and weaknesses

- Identify training that will be available to fill skill gaps

- Take advantage of the change to develop new skills and grow professionally

- Begin to "let go" of the status quo

Choices after the change is implemented

Choices that typically have a *negative* outcome after the change is implemented:

- Avoid using the new work processes or tools whenever possible

- Tell peers or subordinates that using the new work processes or tools is not a big deal and shouldn't be taken too seriously

- Talk negatively about the organization with customers

- Revert to the old way of doing work when problems or issues arise with the change

- Take advantage of problems during implementation to argue why the change will never work

- Complain about the decision to make the change

Choices that typically have a *positive* outcome after the change is implemented:

- Reinforce the change with peers and subordinates

- Help the business achieve the objectives of the change (be results-oriented)

- Avoid reverting back to old processes or ways of doing work when problems arise with the new processes and systems; be patient

- Help solve problems that arise with new work processes and tools

What are the consequences of not changing?

The consequences to you of not changing depend on how critical the change is to the business and your role. For changes that are less critical to business success or that do not directly impact you, the consequences may be minimal. However, if you elect not to support the change, and the change is critical to the success of the organization, the possible consequences are:

- Loss of employment

- Reassignment or transfer with the potential for lower pay

- Lost opportunities for promotion or advancement in the organization

- Reduced job satisfaction as you fight the organization and the organization fights you

What are the benefits of supporting the change?

The benefits of supporting the change, especially a change that is critical to the success of the organization, include:

- Enhanced respect and reputation within the organization

- Improved growth opportunities (especially for active supporters of the change)

- Increased job satisfaction (knowing you are helping your organization respond effectively to a rapidly changing marketplace)

- Improved job security

What if I disagree with the change or I feel they are fixing the wrong problem?

Be patient. Keep an open mind. Make sure you understand the business reasons for the change. However, don't be afraid to voice your specific objections or concerns. If your objections are valid, chances are good they will come to light and be resolved. If you feel strongly against a specific element of the change, let the right people know and do it in an appropriate manner.

What if they've tried before and failed?

The history of your company may include some previous change projects that failed. If failure is what employees are accustomed to, the organization will have a hard time erasing the past. In order for companies to be successful, everyone must be prepared to accept the past as history and focus on what lies ahead.

What if I am forced to do more for the same pay?

When your organization is undergoing a change, this usually means that new processes, systems or skills are required. Your role in the changed environment may include learning these new processes or acquiring new skills. Indeed, some of your responsibilities may change.
For the old way of doing things, compensation may actually decrease as the value of that work to the organization goes down. However, compensation for new work may increase as the value for new services and products increases. This is a part of change.

About the authors

Jeff Hiatt is the founder and lead editor of the Change Management Learning Center (www.change-management.com), author of the books *The Perfect Change* and the *Employee's Survival Guide to Change*, and co-author of *Winning with Quality*. Jeff has led research projects with more than 1000 companies on change management and business process design. He trains on change management and coaches business leaders world-wide. Jeff lives in Colorado with his wife and two children.

Tim Creasey is a senior editor, contributor, and lead research analyst for the Change Management Learning Center. Tim spearheaded the most recent change management benchmarking study with more than 280 companies from 51 countries. Tim lives in Boston with his wife where he is pursuing his MBA at Boston University.